The activist teaching profession

Judyth Sachs

Open University Press

Open University Press
McGraw-Hill Education
McGraw-Hill House
Shoppenhangers Road
Maidenhead
Berkshire
SL6 2QL
United Kingdom.

Email: enquiries@openup.co.uk
World wide web: www.openup.co.uk

and
Two Penn Plaza
New York, NY 10121-2289, USA

First Published 2003. Reprinted 2004

A catalogue record of this book is available from the British Library

ISBN   0 335 20818 5 (pb)   0 335 20819 3 (hb)

Library of Congress Cataloging-in-Publication Data
Sachs, Judyth, 1954-
     The activist teaching profession / Judyth Sachs.
        p. cm. – (Professional learning)
     Includes bibliographical references and index.
     ISBN 0-335-20818-5 (pb) – ISBN 0-335-20819-3 (hb)
     1. Teachers–In-service training.   2. Professional socialization.   I. Title.
II. Series.
LB1731.S23 2002
370'.71'5–dc21   2002072514

Typeset by Graphicraft Limited, Hong Kong
Printed in Great Britain by The Cromwell Press Limited,
Trowbridge, Wiltshire.

The activist teaching profession

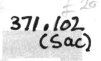

Professional Learning

Series Editors: Ivor Goodson and Andy Hargreaves

The work of teachers has changed significantly in recent years and now, more than ever, there is a pressing need for high-quality professional development. This timely new series examines the actual and possible forms of professional learning, professional knowledge, professional development and professional standards that are beginning to emerge and be debated at the beginning of the twenty-first century. The series will be important reading for teachers, teacher educators, staff developers and policy-makers throughout the English-speaking world.

Published and forthcoming titles:

For TFS and GMS

Contents

Series editors' preface

Teaching today is increasingly complex work, requiring the highest standards of professional practice to perform it well (Hargreaves and Goodson 1996). It is the core profession, the key agent of change in today's knowledge society. Teachers are the midwives of that knowledge society. Without them, or their competence, the future will be malformed and stillborn. In the United States, George W. Bush's educational slogan has been to leave no child behind. What is clear today in general, and in this book in particular, is that leaving no child behind means leaving no teacher or leader behind either. Yet, teaching too is also in crisis, staring tragedy in the face. There is a demographic exodus occuring in the profession as many teachers in the ageing cohort of the Boomer generation are retiring early because of stress, burnout or disillusionment with the impact of years of mandated reform on their lives and work. After a decade of relentless reform in a climate of shaming and blaming teachers for perpetuating poor standards, the attractiveness of teaching as a profession has faded fast among potential new recruits.

Teaching has to compete much harder against other professions for high calibre candidates than it did in the last period of mass recruitment – when able women were led to feel that only nursing and secretarial work were viable options. Teaching may not yet have reverted to being an occupation for 'unmarriageable women and unsaleable men' as Willard Waller described it in 1932, but many American inner cities now run their school systems on high numbers of uncertified teachers. The teacher recruitment crisis in England has led some schools to move to a four-day week; more and more schools are run on the increasingly casualized labour of temporary teachers from overseas, or endless supply teachers whose quality busy administrators do not always have time to monitor (Townsend 2001). Meanwhile in the

Canadian province of Ontario, in 2001, hard-nosed and hard-headed reform strategies led in a single year to a decrease in applications to teacher education programmes in faculties of education by 20–25 per cent, and a drop in a whole grade level of accepted applicants.

Amid all this despair and danger though, there remains great hope and some reason for optimism about a future of learning that is tied in its vision to an empowering, imaginative and inclusive vision for teaching as well. The educational standards movement is showing visible signs of over-reaching itself as people are starting to complain about teacher shortages in schools, and the loss of creativity and inspiration in classrooms (Hargreaves *et al.* 2001). There is growing international support for the resumption of more humane middle years philosophies in the early years of secondary school that put priority on community and engagement, alongside curriculum content and academic achievement. School districts in the United States are increasingly seeing that high quality professional development for teachers is absolutely indispensable to bringing about deep changes in student achievement (Fullan 2001). In England and Wales, policy documents and White Papers are similarly advocating more 'earned autonomy', and freedom from curriculum constraints and inspection requirements, where schools and teachers are performing well (e.g. DfES 2001). Governments almost everywhere are beginning to speak more positively about teachers and teaching – bestowing honour and respect where blame and contempt had prevailed in the recent past.

The time has rarely been more opportune or more pressing to think more deeply about what professional learning, professional knowledge and professional status should look like for the new generation of teachers who will shape the next three decades of public education. Should professional learning accompany increased autonomy for teachers, or should its provision be linked to the evidence of demonstrated improvements in pupil achievement results? Do successful schools do better when the professional learning is self-guided, discretionary and intellectually challenging, while failing schools or schools in trouble benefit from required training in the skills that evidence shows can raise classroom achievement quickly? And does accommodating professional learning to the needs of different schools and their staffs constitute administrative sensitivity and flexibility (Hopkins *et al.* 1997), or a kind of professional development apartheid (Hargreaves, forthcoming)? These are the kinds of questions and issues which this series on professional learning sets out to address. This is why we as editors have been so keen to include Judyth Sachs' book on the activist view of teaching professionalism.

Judyth Sachs provides an invigorating commentary on the fast-changing map of teacher professionalism in the past decade. One of the most pressing concerns for those interested in the changing map of teacher professionalism is the distinction between old professionalism and new professionalism.

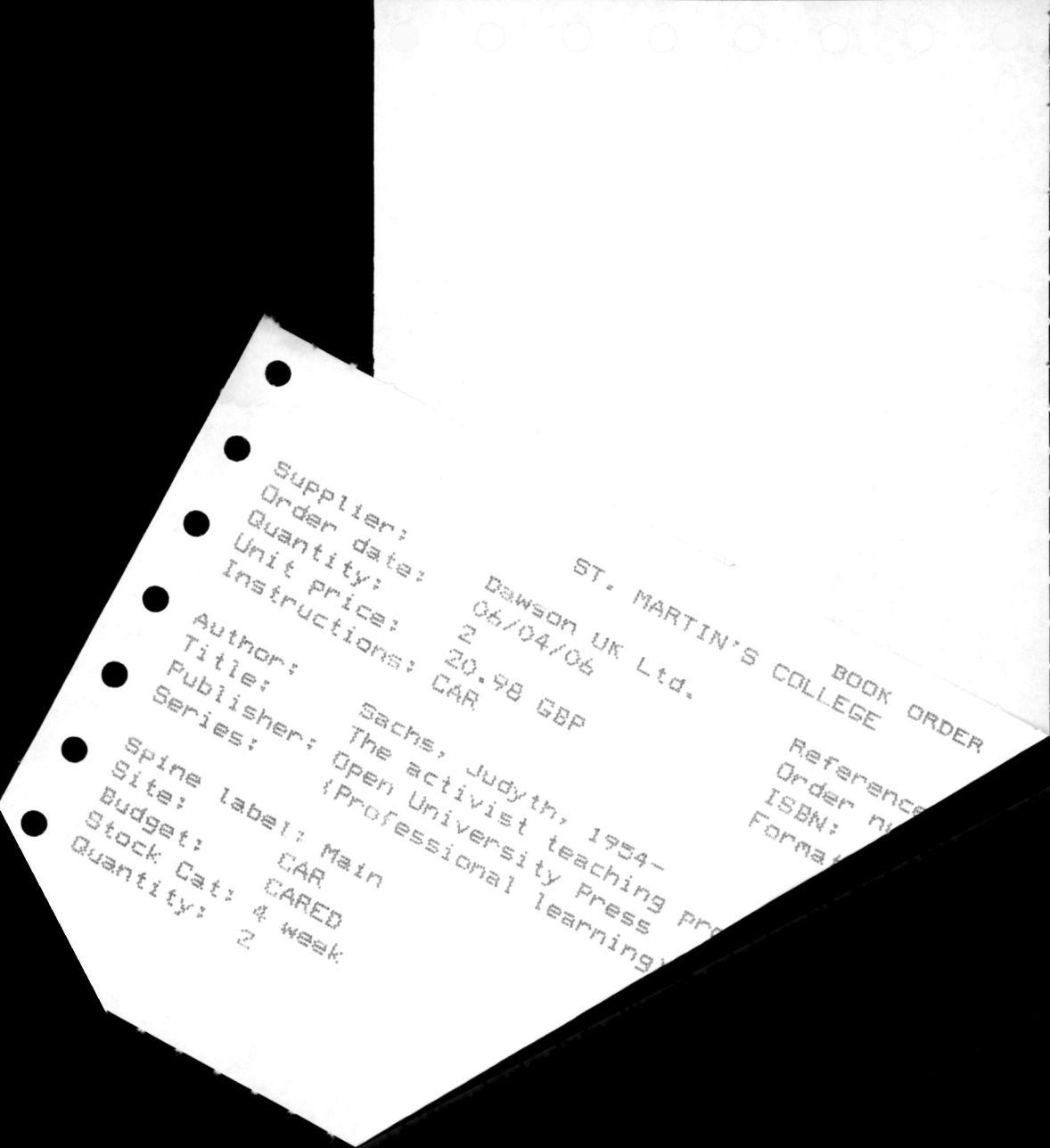

ST. MARTIN'S COLLEGE   BOOK ORDER

Supplier: Dawson UK Ltd.
Order date: 06/04/06
Quantity: 2
Unit Price: 20.98 GBP
Instructions: CAR

Author: Sachs, Judyth, 1954-
Title: The activist teaching pro
Publisher: Open University Press
Series: (Professional learning

Reference
Order n
ISBN:
Forma

Spine label: Main
Site:
Budget: CAR
Stock Cat: CARED
Quantity: 2

Site: ...
Quantity: 4 week

This distinction has been articulated by a number of scholars, most notably Geoff Troman[1].

Sachs uses the division between old and new professionals to locate the debate about the nature of teacher professionalism and behind this the nature of the ethical and moral underpinnings of teacher professionalism. This debate is relatively neglected in a lot of the reformist incantations about professional change, professional standards and professional learning and, as such, it is an important and indeed vital contribution to the ongoing struggle to establish meaningful concepts of teacher professionalism in a fast-changing educational world.

Sachs' analysis is far from being a retrospective 'golden-age' reincantation of old professional standards. The book provides many cutting edge examples of what she calls 'transformative professionalism'. These provide new contexts where activist teaching professionals can rework and rejuvenate the new professional contexts and practices that are now being developed and established. So, far from static retrospection, what we have here is a futurist analysis which aims to provide alternative ways to reconceptualize and rethink notions of teacher professionalism. This is a pressing and imperative mission at this time of change and one which Judyth Sachs pulls off with great dexterity and vision. In the New World of audit cultures and accountability strategies, what is often left out is a clear sense of the social and moral visions and missions which underpin professional teaching. It is almost as if the debate assumes professionalism whilst providing a series of micro-managed strategies and reforms which, in the absence of the analysis of professionalism, may well have the effect of eroding notions of professional visions and ideals of caring vocationalism. This is not a mistake that Sachs will allow us to continue with and a close reading of the book provides many resources for hope and action in the changing world of teaching.

Andy Hargreaves
Ivor Goodson

Note

1 Troman, G. (1996) The rise of the new professionals? the restructuring of primary teachers' work and professionalism, *British Journal of Sociology of Education*, 17(4): 473–87.

References

DfES (Department for Education and Skills) (2001) *Achieving Success*. London: HMSO.

Fullan, M. (2001) *Leading in a Culture of Change*. San Francisco: Jossey-Bass/ Wiley.

Hargreaves, A. (forthcoming) *Teaching in the Knowledge Society*. New York: Teachers College Press.

Hargreaves, A. and Goodson, I. (1996) Teachers' professional lives: aspirations and actualities, in I. Goodson and A. Hargreaves (eds) *Teachers' Professional Lives*. New York: Falmer Press.

Hargreaves, A., Earl, L., Moore, S. and Manning, S. (2001) *Learning to Change: Beyond Teaching Subjects and Standards*. San Francisco: Jossey-Bass/Wiley.

Hopkins, D., Harris, A. and Jackson, D. (1997) Understanding the schools capacity for development: growth states and strategies, *School Leadership and Management*, 17(3): 401–11.

Townsend, J. (2001) It's bad – trust me, I teach there, *Sunday Times*, 2 December.

Waller, W. (1932) *The Sociology of Teaching*. New York: Russell & Russell.

Acknowledgements

This book is the outcome of research and professional activities with teachers in schools in various states in Australia over the period 1995 to 2000. It is the professionalism of these people and the collective work undertaken with many teachers that has enabled the activist work described here to be done. I want to thank the teachers in primary and secondary schools whose practices have demonstrated that alternative ways of thinking about and working in classrooms are possible, even in systems which appear to be conservative and resistant to change. I salute your courage and commitment to the teaching profession.

I also want to acknowledge the part played by my friend and mentor Lloyd Logan whose generosity of spirit and comradeship gave me the courage to take risks in terms of the development of my own research interests and my career.

My postgraduate students have been critical readers of earlier versions of the various chapters of this book. To them I express my thanks and gratitude for keeping me honest. To Julie Steiner and Susan Groundwater Smith I am grateful for reading the manuscript and giving me feedback and encouragement to get it finished. Finally, I thank Anita West for her patience. I am sure that she was relieved when the *Activist Teaching Profession* was completed.

one

Teacher professionalism in transition

The idea of professionals and professionalism has such common currency in everyday language that the explanatory power of these concepts is becoming meaningless. At a time when real estate agents refer to themselves as professionals, window cleaners claim that they provide professional service and sellers of used cars celebrate a professional code of practice, we are left asking what relevance does the concept have for teachers individually and collectively? This book has as its project a critical examination of teacher professionalism, as it is emerging in western societies in general and Australia in particular.

My interest in the area has developed from a long-standing association with schools, education bureaucracies and universities in the generation of policy and my participation in various forms of education practice. My involvement in several teacher professional development projects in Australia has provided me with opportunities to work with teachers in schools across several states. In these projects I have worked as a consultant, as a university-based colleague working with teachers in schools, and as a member of a national advisory committee. These experiences have provided me with the incentive to rethink the practice and possibilities of teacher professionalism from the dual perspectives of an insider and an outsider. As a result, I see the broader project of renewing teacher professionalism as a strategy for systems, unions and individual teachers to rethink the work of teachers while at the same time challenging the public perception of the contribution that teachers make to the social and cultural fabric of society.

This book celebrates and honours the work of teachers and the teaching profession. We are living in times when all of the professions are under a critical public gaze and where issues of standards, accountability and quality of provision or service stand at the core of criticisms of doctors, lawyers as well as teachers. At such times of increasing public scrutiny it is important to look behind the cant and explore what are the factors shaping the issues of what it means for teachers to be professionals and what it means to belong to the teaching profession.

This is particularly important when there are contradictory messages about the quality of teachers employed in the public system and the standard of children's learning outcomes are criticized in the media almost every day. Recent editorials in Australian newspapers have chastised governments for their lack of expenditure on education and on the training and development of teachers. Paradoxically, this is happening at a time when a shortage of qualified teachers is either looming or already exists in Australia, the UK and the USA and when Australian teachers are being actively recruited by employment agencies in the UK, New Zealand and the USA.

The intent of this book is to create discussion among various constituencies interested in the teaching profession and its role and responsibilities in a rapidly changing and complex society. The primary focus is on examining debates currently circulating in the scholarly literature and policies and practices relating to teacher professionalism. Its purpose is twofold: first, to provoke a review of the role and standing of the teaching profession in societies that are rapidly changing and where there are competing claims to limited resources, and second, to provide some strategies for how this might be achieved through the development of an alternative form of teacher professionalism.

The perspective of the book is inherently sociological. To this end it focuses attention on that which is taken for granted, and takes as problematic, concepts such as teacher professionalism, teacher education and teacher professional identity and their inherent practices. Accordingly, the intent is to provide a rigorous analysis of the situations in which these terms are used and the practices that emerge in terms of their various uses.

While I attempt to make this book relevant to a broad international readership by illustrating points with examples from policy and practice in the UK and USA, the book has its genesis and roots in my experience as an Australian educator and academic. Nevertheless, many of the ideas and principles are generalizable across international and linguistic borders and can be taken up and modified to suit specific conditions by teachers, academics and other interested parties. Lest the criticism be made that the focus here is on Australian exceptionalism, the conditions that have facilitated the development of interest in revitalizing teacher professionalism by the teaching profession itself and other interested stakeholders are not unique to the Australian setting. For example, issues of teacher professional standards, the use of practitioner research as a form of teacher professional development and the broad pressures of accountability on social institutions are not unique to Australia. The literature I draw upon and the examples used from Singapore and the USA indicate that other countries are responding to these issues in similar ways.

The chapters that comprise the book take issue with various debates that are shaping policies and practices in Australia, the UK and USA. In order to provide some conceptual coherence, six questions are posed which provide a framework for structuring the book and for developing my argument. These are:

1 What forms of professionalism are shaping the teaching profession?
2 What are the differences between the old and new professionalism?
3 Why is professionalism an important concept for the teaching profession?
4 What conditions and contexts facilitate one form of teacher professionalism over another?
5 What are the tensions and sites of struggle that are shaping the discourses and practices of teacher professionalism?
6 What are some alternative ways to rethink and revitalize the concept and practice of teacher professionalism so that it is relevant to the needs and aspirations of teachers working in increasingly difficult and constantly changing work environments?

In this chapter, I differentiate between old and emerging formations of teacher professionalism. The argument made is that two versions of teacher professionalism are currently circulating in public and scholarly discourse, these are the 'old professionalism' and the 'new professionalism'. These versions of teacher professionalism stand in contradistinction to one another and have emerged in response to particular social, political, economic and cultural conditions. What makes current debates in the area of teacher professionalism seem contradictory is that versions of both the old and new teacher professionalism are being used by teachers themselves and by various education stakeholders in their deliberations about industrial and professional matters. Indeed, teacher professionalism has itself become a site of struggle of ideology over meaning. I propose that the division between old and new professionalism sees these forms of professionalism working against each other. What is happening is a tension of opposites which is both subtle and complex at the same time. Rather than being polar there are overlaps between these old and new forms. I propose that a more accurate way to conceptualize current forms of teacher professionalism is to make a distinction between, on the one hand, old, and on the other, emerging, forms of teacher professionalism: what I refer to as 'transformative professionalism'.

In Chapter 2, the focus is on changes in education policy at the national level in Australia that facilitated the emergence of new forms of teacher professionalism. The impact of public sector management reform in Australia and elsewhere has provoked rigorous debate and various strategies about teacher professional development and teacher professionalism.

Debates and practices of teacher professionalism have a strong political dimension to them. Struggles between various educational interest groups have galvanized around issues of teacher professional standards, what constitutes them, their purpose and their effects. In Chapter 3, teacher professional standards are examined, as is the effect that the development of frameworks of professional standards has on the teaching profession. Again the intent is to look behind some of the claims that are made by those who are strong advocates of the implementation of professional standards across the teaching profession.

Developing new forms of teacher initial training stands at the core of developing new forms of professionalism and professional identity among teachers. Changing forms of social and professional association between teachers and various education interest groups have to be carefully considered and nurtured. The complexity of the competing needs and the possibilities for conflict of interest and misunderstandings regarding what is seen to be in the best interests of teachers and their students all have to be carefully negotiated. Indeed, cooperation between various stakeholders and collaboration among teachers can be a veritable minefield. Chapter 4 examines some of the challenges confronting university-based teacher education programmes and indicates how faculties of education can be responsive by demonstrating strategic leadership to the changing needs of the teaching profession. In order to provide some future-oriented perspective, a framework for a teacher education programme is developed to prepare activist teacher professionals. Furthermore, some strategies are identified that will facilitate the intellectual professional leadership that teacher educators can offer the profession as they respond to the continuing pressures to prepare competent and effective teachers in classrooms.

Developing new forms of teacher professionalism demands the development of new skills by teachers. In order to move beyond old forms of teacher professionalism the work of teaching needs to be redefined. This is not only in terms of skills required in classrooms to ensure effective learning outcomes by students, but also in terms of the needs of teachers as adult learners. Chapter 5 advocates the importance of teacher research as a vehicle for the professional development of teachers and as a strategy for making public and developing the knowledge base of teaching.

In Chapter 6, the practice of professionalism is illustrated through various examples of teacher professional development projects in Australia, the USA and Singapore. In Australia, the Innovative Links between Schools and Universities Project for Teacher Professional Development and various other projects undertaken under the aegis of the National Schools Network provide evidence for system- and school-based teacher professional development.

These projects provide examples of large-scale teacher professional development projects which have been significant in mobilizing groups of teachers, academics, unions and education authorities with the common purpose of renewing and revitalizing teacher professionalism. The Coalition of Essential Schools in the USA and the Teachers' Network in Singapore also have as one of their major goals renewing the teaching profession.

Changing educational policies and practices have challenged images and the understanding of what it means to be a teacher. In Chapter 7, teacher professional identity is put under the microscope. Two forms of teacher professional identity are presented: the entrepreneurial and the activist. I argue that these two forms of teacher professional identity emerge in response to the current discourses circulating and informing education policy.

These chapters contribute to the development of a new type of teacher professional who is working towards the broad agenda of the activist teacher professional. Chapter 8 brings together some of the issues regarding the politics of teacher professionalism and education policy, teacher professional identity and examples of successful professional development projects. In this final chapter I propose a strategy to help to rebuild public trust and interest in the teaching profession and to mobilize teachers so that they can be in control of the agenda for reclaiming the terrain of teacher professionalism.

Teacher professionalism: old and transformative formations

Debates about the meaning of teacher professionalism, its purposes and whether or not teaching can be defined as a profession circulate in scholarly and public debates with great regularity. Some of these debates serve purely ideological interests, especially when their focus is on arguing that teaching should not be designated a profession. These interests, usually the state and employing authorities, are concerned with controlling teachers individually and collectively by specifying the skills, competencies and attributes of teachers along narrow technicist lines. Others have strongly advocated that teaching is a profession and provided strong evidence in support of such claims. These debates have used a variety of theoretical orientations and positions. Some have drawn on Marxist theory (Larson 1977), whereas others provide a more functionalist theoretical perspective (Hoyle and John 1995). Some academic writers (Hargreaves and Goodson 1996; Hargreaves 2000) have developed typologies about the various discourses of teacher professionalism or have identified historical phases of teacher professionalism. It is not my purpose here to re-rehearse these debates, this has been done by others (Ozga and Lawn 1981; Hargreaves and Goodson 1996; Helsby 1999), nor am I attempting to engage with debates about what constitutes a profession, the process of professionalization or the general area of professionalism. I take as given Hargreaves' (2000: 152) claim that:

> Outside education, professions have been represented theoretically, in the image of those who belong to them, and who advance their interests as having a strong technical culture with a specialized knowledge base and shared standards of practice, a service ethic, long periods of training, and high degrees of autonomy.

For my purposes here, first and foremost, the focus is on teacher professionalism and not on debates about whether or not teaching is or is not a profession. Second is the view that teacher professionalism as a concept or as a political project is not static but, rather, that new forms of teacher professionalism are emerging in response to changing social, economic and political conditions. Finally, it is teachers themselves in concert with various interested stakeholders who must make the intellectual, political and social running when it comes to strategies to enhance the work of teachers and the perception of the importance and status of teachers within the wider community.

I take the view that to seek a fixed position is futile: professionalism has always been a changing concept rather than a generic one (Freidson 1994). Furthermore, I see the concept and practice of professionalism as a site of struggle, especially as it relates to meaning.

> Professionalism is currently an area of struggle between important actors within Great Britain and the Anglo-American world. . . . This struggle revolves around whose definition of professionalism emerges as hegemonic and therefore who has access to significant economic resources.
>
> (Hanlon 1998: 48)

The lack of consensus regarding what constitutes teacher professionalism cannot be underestimated, especially if the broader political and social strategy is to revitalize teacher professionalism. As Hargreaves and Goodson (1996: 4) argue:

> What it means to be professional, to show professionalism or to pursue professionalization is not universally agreed or understood . . . what counts as professional knowledge and professional action in teaching is open to many interpretations.

Given that the field has already been quite extensively mined, it is not my intention to provide yet another review of the literature. Instead I take as my focus the distinction between what has been differentiated as 'old' and 'new' forms of teacher professionalism (Troman 1996). 'Old' forms of teacher professionalism draw on established studies of professionalism and professionalization in order to argue the case of teaching as a profession. Alternatively, 'new' teacher professionalism takes into account previous debates about teacher professionalism but assumes a changed analytical perspective from which to understand professionalism (McLaughlin 1997). Here notions of teacher professionalism are being redefined in what Hargreaves (2000: 153) describes as more positive and principled post-modern ways that are flexible, wide-ranging and inclusive in nature.

There is still much discussion about the old and new formations of teacher professionalism, and debates regarding the concept and practice of professionalism. Given that these debates circulate around issues of power and status, this is likely to continue. As Grace (1987: 195) observes:

> Ideologies of professionalism can be made to serve the interests of the state for control and containment of teachers or they can be effectively deployed by teachers to improve their terms and conditions of service and their enjoyment of social status and occupational autonomy.

For some, the work of teachers is being deprofessionalized (Apple 1982) through the application of managerialist policies aimed at increasing the public accountability of teachers individually and collectively. Others (McCulloch *et al.* 2000: 110) argue that professions in general are changing, with teaching becoming more professional and that evidence of this can be seen across the world. They maintain that:

> occupations such as teaching are becoming more professional, new skills are required, achieving good relationships with client and other stakeholders becomes more important, a more extensive knowledge base has to be mastered and more complex decisions need to be made. Rather than being deprofessionalized, it could be argued that teaching is being reprofessionalized although the new professionalism is different from the mythical professionalism of forty years ago.
>
> (McCulloch *et al.* 2000: 110)

The differences between the old and new formations of teacher professionalism are many. The politics of professionalism are partly about government action that affects teachers, but they are also about the ways in which teachers choose to respond and to depict themselves. Discussion of 'new professionalism' as well as 'old professionalism' shows that there is a choice (McCulloch *et al.* 2000).

In what follows I elaborate some of the dimensions of old teacher professionalism and what I prefer to call 'transformative' teacher professionalism. These two types of teacher professionalism are not necessarily diametrically opposed, there are some areas where dimensions of teacher professionalism overlap, or there is a lack of clarity because of the emerging nature of issues that are affecting the teaching profession.

Old teacher professionalism

Conceptions of old teacher professionalism have had wide currency in the educational literature as well as in popular discourse. In general, old versions of professionalism have been concerned with identifying attributes of a profession and locating various occupational groups within discrete categories, such as law, medicine, engineering etc. Larson (1977), for example, demonstrated how elite professions such as medicine and law in particular have been able to create a market for their services and establish who is competent to be a member of the group by controlling entry standards, as well as the conditions for continuing membership, by dictating continuing education, registration and so on. Through these activities these professions establish the boundaries for inclusion and exclusion, while at the same time they are able to achieve a mandate for the exclusive supply of these services. This strategy is reinforced by creating an ideology of professionalism which in turn enhances their status. In this instance, as Freidson (1986) argues, professions are a phenomenon of labour market organization. They are those occupations exercising the capacity to 'create exclusive shelters in the labour market for accepted practitioners through the monopolization of educational training and credentials required for the attainment of economic opportunities in the market' (Brint 1994: 262).

While the elite professions have been more active in this kind of professionalism, members of the teaching profession, especially through teacher professional associations, such as subject associations, have been engaged in a similar professionalizing strategy. For our purposes, professions are 'occupations that the higher education system chooses to treat as requiring advanced formal training and for which no acceptable training exists outside of the higher education system' (Brint 1994: 263).

Current orthodoxy suggest that, for teachers, three areas encapsulate what it means to be professional and hence professionalism. These are knowledge, autonomy and responsibility (Hoyle and John 1995). These three dimensions work together in complex and reciprocal ways; none stands independently of any other. While Lortie (1975) and Jackson (1968) argue that teachers lack both a technical vocabulary and a corpus of knowledge about their practice, more recent research has emphasized the body of knowledge that teachers possess in order to carry out their work as teachers. This knowledge has been variously described as personal practical knowledge (Clandinin and Connelly 1988, 1995), practical knowledge (Elbaz 1983) or pedagogical content knowledge (Shulman 1986). More recently, Putnam and Borko (1997) have focused on the role of teachers' knowledge and beliefs. They make the point that 'a teacher's knowledge and beliefs – about learning, teaching and subject matter – are critically important determinants of how a teacher teaches'.

Larson (1993: 12) makes the important point that 'every profession claims to be based on knowledge produced culture: not in its specialized body of knowledge and in its canon only, but also in its codified practices, its explicit and implicit norms, its ways of making sense of rules and legitimising practices'. Regardless of its nomenclature, each of these perspectives has been able to provide empirical evidence that supports claims that teachers possess a cogent body of knowledge that they apply in classrooms, working with students. This is a body of expert knowledge that enables them to make judgements about student learning and their own performance as teachers.

An ongoing challenge is for teachers and others involved in education to make the knowledge base of teaching an essential part of the professional project. Once this is achieved the knowledge base may become a central resource of the profession, and will remain so as long as the profession can maintain its exclusive right to it (Macdonald 1995). This is a significant point because it is the acquisition and possession of this knowledge that differentiates the knowledge base of teachers from those who can best be described as working in the field of training. The knowledge base of teaching is of direct importance, consisting as it does of a codified or codifiable aggregation of knowledge, skill, understanding and technology of ethics and a disposition of collective responsibility (Shulman 1986: 4).

Practitioner autonomy is another dimension that is seen to be central to a profession. The autonomous discourse of a profession is inclusive of the knowledge and justifications it produces by and for itself (Larson 1993). For Hoyle and John (1995: 77), 'as professionals work in uncertain situations in which judgement is more important than routine, it is essential to effective practice that they should be free from bureaucratic and political constraints to act on judgements made in the best interests (as they see them) of the clients'. A countervailing argument suggests that accountability often stands in contradistinction to autonomy. Hoyle and John (1995: 77) claim that 'professional practice is more predictable and subject to evaluation than professional interest groups allow, and their claims for autonomy are, in fact, strategies for avoidance of accountability and the involvement of clients in dialogue about practice'.

Given the increasing regimes of accountability and verification that affect all people working in the professions, it is no longer useful to place accountability and autonomy in opposition. The issues now might be, what forms do the systems of accountability take, who oversees their application and what are the consequences if transgression is seen to happen. In the case of teaching in Australia, there is currently no national organization to certify programmes or to register individual teachers. The British, Australian or American Medical Association come to mind as professional organizations that provide this function. In some states in Australia and the USA there are

teacher standards and registration bodies that provide guidelines and procedures for entrance and continuing membership of the profession. In the
UK, visits by Ofsted inspectors play a role in assuring quality at the school
level so that, in this instance, accountability has both structural and professional dimensions. The intrusion on teachers' personal autonomy is more
likely to come from a centralized and mandated curriculum and the publication of students' results in public examinations rather than from intervention
that aims specifically to reduce that autonomy.

Responsibility and professionality go hand in hand, and there are three
levels: the practical level, the exercise of sound judgement, and being
equipped to make sound judgements through professional development,
ethics and reflection (Hoyle and John 1995). The practical level is concerned
with the possession of knowledge that enables teachers to undertake their
work in classrooms competently. The exercise of sound judgement draws
on the complex body of knowledge developed by teachers and mediated
through their experience in classrooms, and their understanding of content
and pedagogical knowledge. The acquisition of this knowledge is dependent
on teachers being involved in various forms of professional development, of
which taking up opportunities to be engaged in learning and dialogue with
other teachers inside and outside of schools is central.

In its application, the proponents of old professionalism have an ideological commitment to the very notion of teacher professionalism. Brint
(1994: 7) suggests that:

> professionalism has both a technical and moral aspect. Technically,
> it promised competent performance of skilled work involving the
> application of broad and complex knowledge, the acquisition of which
> required formal academic study. Morally, it promised to be guided by
> the application of the important social ends it served.

The identification of technical and moral aspects of professionalism is,
not surprisingly, attractive to large segments of society, especially policy-
makers and members of the profession itself. Hoyle and John (1995: 7)
observe that the ideological approach 'denotes a much more political set of
activities in which the concept of profession is deployed in a deliberate
attempt to influence policy'. They go on to argue that 'status is seen as a
function of power which has accrued to a profession through increasing
control of the market' (1995: 7). The spheres of interest in which proponents of old professionalism operate are, in the main, concerned with the
profession itself and are inward-looking and exclusive.

Spheres of interest are concerned with power and the privileges of professionals that grow out of the specific character of their market shelter.
These spheres of interest operate through various strategies and structural
arrangements, including knowledge monopolies, gatekeeping functions and

certification (Freidson 1986). Knowledge monopolies create the basis for a great many of the powers of professionals, in particular how their work is to be accomplished. Control over their work, or technical autonomy, is a fundamental aspect of professionals. Technical autonomy creates a sphere of activity in which the individual worker, not the organized hierarchy, is sovereign under normal conditions. It allows for forms of self-direction that are clearly not open to all workers (Brint 1994).

Gatekeeping ensures institutional power over resources. These resources may take a variety of forms, from entry into the profession, to the allocation of promotional positions within the profession, to the allocation of grades as a measure of performance. As Brint (1994) observes, gatekeeping defines a position of interpretation and judgement between a client and a benefit a client seeks. In the case of teachers, it is only they who can give grades that measure performance and codify learning outcomes.

The major constituency of membership for those operating under an old professionalism is exclusive, limited mainly to those working in the field of school education in the capacity of teacher, administrator, union officer or education bureaucrat. It is unlikely that community members, even teacher educators or those working in allied education fields, would be included under the old professional project. Its focus is on the needs of teachers as an identifiable group, especially as these relate to the immediate and practical needs of teachers working in classrooms.

Old forms of teacher professionalism can run the risk of serving particular interests to the neglect of others. It is often self-serving and inward-looking, insufficiently concerned with broad social and political issues. Bottery and Wright (2000: 100) put it well when they suggest that:

> A teaching profession of limited rationality and similarly limited professionalism not only serves controversial political and economic ends. It is also limited in its ability to develop a generation that can adequately respond to the complex and changing demands of a more global environment, as well as to provide the sorts of skills and attitudes required for a more empowered and participative citizenry.

Often when professional groups come under sustained external political attack there is a tendency for them to become self-serving, self-referential and self-justifying. The test of a mature profession is to be able to be able to engage in self-reflective moments in order to counter the possibility of the truth of such claims and at the same time have strategies in place in order to prevent such critics from emerging.

In summary, old professionalism is characterized by the following:

- exclusive membership
- conservative practices
- self-interest

- external regulation
- slow to change
- reactive.

I argue that the old professional formations are no longer appropriate for a redefined teaching profession. New times, different challenges combined with conditions of uncertainty and ambiguity, require alternative ways of thinking about and engaging in the work of teaching. Furthermore, new strategies for membership and mobilization for change are also required. An old professionalism does not provide the intellectual or moral leadership of a profession such as teaching in circumstances where being proactive, tactical and strategic are imperative. Under the current policy agendas, an alternative type of teacher professionalism needs to emerge and gain acceptance both inside and outside of the profession; this is what I refer to as transformative professionalism.

Transformative professionalism

Teachers are working in conditions characterized by increased public scrutiny, more sophisticated techniques for ensuring accountability and a myriad of strategies for measuring student learning outcomes. There is increased public interest in education as evidenced in the number of media reports about school successes and failures. In the UK, what could be called public shaming is enacted when schools fail to measure up to Ofsted inspections and when league tables as a measure of performance of schools in public examinations are printed in newspapers. Similar forms of close examination of the public (state, in the UK) schooling system are also happening in Australia, the USA and New Zealand.

The organization of work practices, the use of technology and the types of students that teachers find in front of them in their classrooms require alternative ways of thinking and talking about the teaching profession. Furthermore, the rapid rate of change and the increasing access that students have to knowledge and information through the use of information communication technologies require a different type of teacher professionalism that is more outward looking and responsive than the old formations of teacher professionalism.

Adding to the pressures, stresses and strains caused by these forms of systematic accountability is the fact that the boundaries between the public work of teachers and their private lives are also becoming increasingly blurred, while their private lives are under public scrutiny. There is also growing evidence of intensification of teachers' work, increased stress and dissatisfaction with their work. These conditions have contributed to claims that teachers are being deprofessionalized and contribute to what could be called a crisis of legitimacy of the profession.

Bottery (1996: 179–80) argues that any version of professionalism must be inclusive of *expertise* (the possession by an occupational group of exclusive knowledge and practice), of *altruism* (an ethical concern by this group for its clients), and *autonomy* (the professionals' need and right to exercise control of entry into, and subsequent practice within, that particular occupation). These three features provide the platform for teacher professionalism.

On first glance this is similar to the orthodox, or old, professionalism of Hoyle and John (1995). However, a closer examination reveals altruism, especially as it relates to an ethical concern, as a new dimension. This is an interesting inclusion since many school systems or professional associations have developed codes of conduct or a set of ethics which underpin professional practice. This has often been in response to increasing regimes of accountability or, in other instances, as a risk management strategy to both protect and enhance the quality of provision by the organization.

For Bottery (1996), five essential ethics inform teacher professionalism, which I would suggest is a transformative teacher professionalism. These are:

- An *ethic of truth disclosure* which must override personal advantage.
- An *ethic of subjectivity* for each individual must recognize the limits of his or her perceptions, the individuality of his or her values.
- An *ethic of reflective integrity* as each professional recognizes the limits of personal perception, of the need to incorporate many understandings of a situation.
- An *ethic of humility* as each professional recognizes that such subjectivity means that personal fallibility is not a failing but a condition of being human.
- An *ethic of humanistic education* of the duty to help the client help themselves.

(Bottery 1996: 193)

Acknowledgment and practice of these ethics provides a strong conceptual as well as political platform for teachers to demonstrate the complexity of their work. They require a rethinking of their role and practice in schools as well as a challenging of some of the taken-for-granted orthodoxies about the nature of professional practice and the role and function of teachers in society.

It is a shift in the social tradition, which David Hargreaves (1994) describes as the culture, values and practices of many teachers, that constitute what he refers to as 'the new professionalism'. Indeed, while the broader social and ideological picture may seem grim, there are emerging opportunities for teachers to renegotiate an alternative form of professionalism. Andy Hargreaves (2000: 176) describes the opportunities that these conditions create:

The forces of de-professionalization in teaching have cut deep. But the objective prospects for a re-invigorated post-modern professionalism, and the creation of a broad social movement that would support it, are strong. If teachers want to become professionally stronger, they must now open themselves up and become more publicly vulnerable and accessible.

Like both Andy Hargreaves and David Hargreaves, McLaughlin (1997) also sees that the new professionalism provides the conditions and the professional spaces for teachers to take responsibility for their own professional lives by engaging in what she refers to as 'practical action'. Implicit in any notion of practical action is the assumption that building teacher professionalism requires new ways of supporting teachers' learning and development. McLaughlin (1997: 89) identifies six principles that provide the conceptual and practical basis for a new professionalism to be established:

- increasing opportunities for professional dialogue;
- reducing teachers' professional isolation;
- providing a rich menu of nested opportunities for learning and discourse;
- connecting professional development opportunities to meaningful content and change efforts;
- creating an environment of professional safety and trust;
- restructuring time, space and scale within schools.

These principles operate at structural and individual levels. In essence, they are concerned with shifting the locus of power away from systemic constraints, such as those enshrined in legislation, regulations and rules, and moving the locus of control to the needs of teachers individually and collectively, operating inside and outside of schools. These principles have substantial effects on how teachers engage in their work in schools and classrooms and how they define that work. For some teachers it requires a substantial shift in their values and practices.

At the centre of this new or transformative professionalism is the need for teachers to understand themselves better and the society in which they live. Bottery (1996) argues that this comes from an understanding of their practice and what would make it more successful. In short it acknowledges the importance of self-knowledge:

[Self-knowledge] allows professionals to assess their weaknesses and strengths that much better. It allows them to appreciate that some justifications are valid, others are little more than rationalizations for historical accident. It allows them to place themselves within a wider picture, and see that sometimes (perhaps often) legislative change may not be aimed at them specifically, but has a wider target, and that they happen to be in the way. It gives them the opportunity to see that they do not necessarily occupy the centre of any occupational universe, but are part of a much more complex ecology of occupations. Professional action can only be enriched by such understandings.

(Bottery 1996: 191)

Transformative professionalism involves not only individual attributes but also a collective strategy on the part of those engaged in any educational enterprise. It means that new forms of work organization are established between teachers, in particular that the hoary chestnut of teacher privatism, isolation and individualism is dispensed with. This isolation and individualism in particular create an environment where teachers resist attempts to confront any of the taken-for-granted aspects of their practice. Its most serious effect is, as Goodlad (1984) argues, a dull routine and homogeneity of practice. Isolation only helps to reinforce conventional and conservative practice. In some respects it can lock teachers into a time warp of their own experiences as students or as neophyte teachers. It limits opportunities to engage in learning and professional dialogue. Moreover, it reinforces a strongly practical and instrumental orientation to the work of teaching, as both an intellectual and a creative activity.

Identifying with transformative professionalism means that teachers will have to work collaboratively, not only with other teachers but also with others interested in education and improving student learning outcomes. Hargreaves (2000) goes so far as to suggest that teachers will have to work with parents and the wider community, arguing that if teachers are to become professionally stronger, they must open themselves up and become publicly vulnerable and accessible. The inclusion of parents into the professional algorithm constitutes one of the dimensions of Hargreaves' postmodern professionalism. According to Hargreaves (2000: 174):

it is in teachers' own interests to treat even imperfect parents not just as irritants or as targets for appeasement, but as the most important allies teachers have in serving those parents' own students and in defending themselves against political assaults on their professionalism.

In many respects there are already strong pockets of teachers whose professional practice is indicative of a transformative professionalism. The differences between old professionalism and transformative professionalism are not as stark as might initially appear. On some dimensions there would be teachers whose own practice and understanding of professionalism falls across or even between the two forms of professionalism presented here. In other instances, teachers' professional practice may be shaped by the contexts in which they are currently working. Indeed, their workplaces may well demand a particular expression of old professionalism while their own preferences may be more towards the transformational. The point I want to emphasize here is that transformative professionalism is not an idealized form of teacher professionalism, but rather one that teachers can feel suits their own needs and fits with their professional aspirations. Importantly, a transformative teacher professionalism is not held together by dogma or fear that 'by not towing the party line' there will be damaging professional consequences. Transformative teacher professionalism needs to be seen by members of the teaching profession as serving the best interests of *all* those interested and participating in schooling and education. In this sense the teaching profession must be strategic and tactical in how it presents itself not only to its own constituency but also in the broader social arena.

In summary, the characteristics of transformative professionalism include:

- inclusive membership
- public ethical code of practice
- collaborative and collegial
- activist orientation
- flexible and progressive
- responsive to change
- self-regulating
- policy-active
- enquiry-oriented
- knowledge-building.

The development of a transformative teacher professionalism questions and criticizes taken-for-granted practices and structures and may well be resisted by the state and its various structures for regulating the teaching profession. For our purposes here, it should also be emphasized that transformative professionalism should not become an orthodoxy which is imposed on the teaching profession. It cannot be emphasized enough that the move for a transformative professionalism must come from the membership of the profession and be supported by other interest groups and stakeholders. This kind of professionalism is activist in its orientation – an idea that is developed in Chapter 8 – and its purpose is to improve the status and conditions of teachers wherever they work. Moreover, it is essential to recognize that the development of this kind of teacher professionalism will take time. While there are many teachers working in educational institutions who are operating as transformative professionals, there are also many teachers who find comfort in old professionalism. To this end, transformative professionalism across the whole profession is something to aspire to and may well take considerable time and energy to achieve. Its singular strength is that it is concerned with mutual engagement around a joint enterprise, namely improving student learning outcomes.

Conclusion

It is clear that the concept of teacher professionalism is not static, nor is it a concept whose meaning is understood or shared by the whole profession. If anything, the term 'teacher professionalism' is a site of struggle over meaning among its various constituencies. Its meaning changes in response to external pressures, public debates and developments in the scholarly field. The debates regarding teacher professionalism are played out in a variety of spheres. These range from the work of professional associations and education unions, to policy statements and debates in the media, especially newspapers. It is paramount that whatever meaning of professionalism is circulating, its meaning is generated and owned by teachers themselves in order that it should have currency among teachers and be useful in improving their public image and social importance.

In this chapter I have distinguished between old professionalism and transformative professionalism, both versions of which are to be found in operation in schools and bureaucracies. There are debates in the media about how the wider community would prefer to define teacher professionalism. My preference is one that supports transformative professionalism; this is based on my experience of working in schools as a teacher, working with teachers in schools as an academic, and as a member of the general public wanting a well-respected and educated teaching force. It is my hope that this book may provoke groups of teachers to rethink their conceptions and practices of teacher professionalism and become part of a groundswell for a transformative teacher professionalism and an activist teaching profession. On the basis of the work being carried out in schools mentioned later in the book, there is strong evidence that a transformative teacher professionalism is possible and that there are active pockets of teachers in the UK, Australia, Singapore and the USA who are exemplars of this at work.

two

Rethinking the practice
of teacher professionalism

Since the early 1990s, various school reform and teacher professional development activities have been implemented across Australia and elsewhere
in response to wide-ranging social and political conditions. In their wake,
teachers working in all kinds of educational institutions have had to respond to a range of challenges at the structural and individual levels. At the
structural level, teachers face the ongoing challenges of pressure of external
accountability from a variety of education stakeholders. There has also
been increased political pressure to direct the processes and provision of
school education, while at the same time there is increasing emphasis on the
delivery of more economically and efficient education provision. Overarching
this is the imperative to prepare students who are numerate, literate and
able to take civic and social responsibility. At the individual level, teachers
are expected to be skilled practitioners who are able to solve immediate
practical problems, are able to reflect on their practice in order to develop
quality learning opportunities for their students, and are able to cope with
rapid change inside and outside of their classrooms.

In this context, rethinking the practice of teacher professionalism can
be viewed as a broad political project that has been seized upon by unions,
government and teacher professional associations alike. In Australia, the
project of reclaiming teacher professionalism had its antecedents in industrial and professional activities during the late 1980s and early 1990s.
Specifically, award restructuring at the federal level during the early 1990s
provided the impetus for school reform and restructuring and the promise of renewed teacher professionalism. The award restructuring period
was one of greater integration of the teacher unions into the wider trade
union movement as other unions took up education and training issues.

For Preston (1996: 165), 'Award restructuring involved a transition from a concern with "macro-industrial" to "micro-industrial" policy; from concern with industry-wide policies to improve productivity and competitiveness to company-level and workplace policies and practices.' She goes on to argue that:

> Award restructuring for teachers was shaped not only by the wider award restructuring industrial agenda, but also by developments in the mid 1980s in Commonwealth–State relations in schooling and industrial relations – a more 'national' approach to schooling developed, and teachers gained access to the Commonwealth industrial relations arena.

Importantly, at this time the development of a national approach to schooling and a rethinking of the industrial agenda for the teaching profession had significant implications for the development of initiatives to enhance teacher professionalism across the country. This rethinking of professional and industrial alignments had long-term effects on educational policy and practice at the national and state levels.

In this chapter I argue that rethinking the practice of teacher professionalism requires a recasting of professional and industrial issues and relationships among employers, unions, teachers and other education stakeholders. Five principles of engagement – learning, participation, collaboration, cooperation and activism – provide a conceptual framework to achieve this. These principles stand at the core of rethinking the practice of teacher professionalism. I use the examples of two Australian national reform initiatives to indicate how these principles have the potential to contribute to the rethinking of teacher professionalism in practice.

The chapter is in three sections. The first identifies the conditions which prompted a rethinking of teacher professionalism in Australia and elsewhere, namely the New Public Management (NPM) or public sector reform. The second section describes the application of NPM to school reform initiatives as they occurred in Australia during the late 1980s and early 1990s. Both of these initiatives were significant in shaping federal and state policy regarding the teaching profession and how the profession would respond to the broader social and political agenda. I argue that two discourses have emerged in response to these conditions and these have shaped definitions and conceptions of teacher professionalism within the teaching profession and outside it. The final section presents a platform that would support the development of a broad strategy to facilitate the rethinking of teacher professionalism inside and outside the profession.

The new public management and reforms of the public sector

The 1980s and 1990s were characterized by a period of significant transformation across the public sector that have had far-reaching effects on
the structures, cultures and practices of its constituent subsections and
individual organizations. Schools too have been affected by these reforms.
As A. Hargreaves (1994: 23) argues:

> the challenges and changes facing teachers and schools are not paro-
> chially confined to education but are rooted in a major socio-historical
> transition from a period of modernity to post modernity. A conse-
> quence of this is that schools and teachers are being affected more and
> more by the demands and contingencies of an increasingly fast paced,
> postmodern world.

Since the 1980s, every feature of the public sector in Australia has under-
gone extensive reform; the cultures, structures and processes bear little
resemblance to those of earlier change initiatives. These reforms are based
on the assumption that the application of market theory and private
sector management principles, procedures and structures to the public
sector will result in increased efficiencies, improved quality of service
and greater accountability.

The central precepts underlying the application of commercial approaches
to the public sector include assumptions that:

1 traditional structures, procedures and services are inefficient;
2 there is a generic set of skills called 'management';
3 private enterprise management approaches are superior to other
   alternatives;
4 managerial and structural reforms guarantee revision to practice that
   results in increased productivity;
5 government services can be quantified for accountability purposes;
6 reform is management led (Sachs and Logan 1997).

Market and managerial theories and strategies are being applied across the
board in the public sector through imperatives of deregulation, performance
monitoring, increased use of mechanisms to measure and codify policy outcomes as well as new measures of accountability. The three tenets of NPM
are *effectiveness*, *efficiency* and *economy*. Effectiveness means managing
change better; efficiency suggests focusing on outcomes and results, while
economy refers to doing more with less. The Organization for Economic
Cooperation and Development (OECD) has noted that the new paradigm
for management has been the creation of a 'performance oriented' and 'less
centralized' public sector with the following characteristics: a focus on results
and efficiency and effectiveness; decentralized management environments;

flexibility to explore alternatives to the public provision of services; establishment of productivity targets and a competitive environment between public sector organizations; and a strengthening of strategic capacities at the centre of the organization (OECD 1995: 8).

Exworthy and Halford (1999: 3) note that:

> Particularly significant changes have included the imposition of new arrangements for financial accountability and the measurement of 'effectiveness', the marketization of structural arrangements, between those who provide welfare services and those who pay for them; and attempts to change established relations between service providers and consumers.

During this period the restructuring of the Australian state has had substantial effects on the character of educational policy, as well as upon the structures and processes of policy production and practice. Taylor *et al.* (1997: 81) argue that 'whereas economic outcomes were once considered to be only one aspect of educational policy, they have now become central'. This has had a substantial effect on the content as well as the intent of educational policy.

Corporate managerialism, devolution and the role of markets are the three key elements of the public sector reform agenda in Australia. Corporate managerialism can best be defined as 'a rational output oriented, plan based and management led view of organizational reform' (Sinclair 1989, quoted in Taylor *et al.* 1997: 81). Devolution has been viewed as a strategy to reduce duplication of activities and costs, and as a way to achieve more predictable and effective outcomes. Its implementation has had a paradoxical effect, for while decisions and to some extent resources are to be devolved, the development of policies remains firmly in the hands of centrally located bureaucrats.

Marketization of education has taken two forms. The first is a commercial strategy whereby schools market themselves and compete with other providers in the marketplace. The second, and much more aligned with the tenets of public sector management reform, sees educational institutions restructuring themselves to reflect the structures of business and industry based on the argument that business processes and structures are more efficient, effective and economical.

A more obvious dimension of marketization of education is the appropriation of the language of business into everyday educational discourse. Kenway *et al.* (1993: 4) observe that:

> The market metaphor heads up a new policy and administrative lexicon in education which includes such terms as *educational property, educational enterprise, entrepreneurial approaches to education, educational services, products, packages, sponsors, commodities and consumers,*

value added education, user pays, choice, competition and so on. These and other terms reflect and are helping to bring into effect, a relatively new and different era into public education in Australia, one in which educational purposes, languages and practices are being subsumed by marketing purposes, languages and practices.

(italics in original)

These strategies become taken for granted and are no longer questioned but, rather, become integrated into the cultures of the central bureaucracies, schools and even classrooms. They become part of the commonsense discourses of schooling and are no longer seen as being problematical or as acting against the best interests of schools or schooling systems. In fact the paradox is that if schools do not take on this discourse they are seen to be out of line with contemporary thinking and policy processes.

The context of rethinking teacher professionalism in Australia

The public sector management reforms described above had a significant impact on strategies for the provision of initial and continuing education of teachers. They had a trickle-down effect not only on the centrally developed policies about teacher professional development and the nature of teacher professionalism but also on industrial debates and consequent policy developments within various education sectors. During the 1980s, issues of teacher professionalism were one of the sites of struggle when Australian industry was restructuring industrial awards. In education, award restructuring fuelled union activity, mobilized professional groups, and unsettled traditional relations between state government education authorities and between state and federal governments in education.

Debate about the relationship between the industrial and professional dimensions of teachers' work, and who represented teachers in those areas, surged into prominence, as did intergovernmental relations and authority (Seddon 1996). However, by 1993, award restructuring had disappeared from the public view. Nevertheless, it left a significant legacy with regard to the development of new types of relationships among the unions, the profession and government, at both state and federal levels. According to Seddon (1996: 3), 'a joint industrial and professional agenda was promoted which affirmed that award restructuring would provide a potent mechanism for reforming the work of teachers, and therefore, the processes of teaching and learning which lie at the heart of education'.

In 1993, the Commonwealth government negotiated a Teaching Accord with the Australian Education Union (AEU) and the Independent Education Union (IEU).[1] The Teaching Accord established priorities and detailed the commitment of the Commonwealth to the involvement of the profession and its financial support for professional development, curriculum assessment and research projects, with seed funding for the National Schools Project and the Australian Teaching Council. According to Sharan Burrow (1996), then president of the Australian Education Union, the Accord encouraged school reform, a move towards professional standards, and some greater salary justice and equity through salary scales across the profession. The Accord was contested and conflictual but, on balance, it provided the teaching profession with useful foundations for the future. Burrow argues that, in particular, 'award restructuring fuelled the further emergence of the education profession and consolidated its determination to take more control over professional life' (Burrow 1996: 114).

These two initiatives created the necessary political conditions within teaching and outside of it to facilitate debate about the nature and scope of teacher professionalism. The watershed for this shift was the Teaching Accord of 1993, which, as the then minister for schools, Ross Free, pointed out, 'constitutes a very tangible recognition of the fundamental role that teachers must play in the continued development of the profession' (quoted in Preston 1996: 190). The Accord and its associated initiatives was later to play a significant part in opening notions of teacher professionalism to discussion by various education industry stakeholders including academics, teachers, bureaucrats working within education systems, as well as professional development agencies and staff working on teacher professional development projects. Indeed, it provided the forum for teacher professionalism to put itself on the political agenda and for the profession to take responsibility for defining itself.

Despite the collapse of the joint union and government initiatives for professional renewal that occurred during the early 1990s, several national initiatives survived which had as their focus the revitalization of teacher professionalism. These were the National Schools Network, an offspring of the National Schools Project, and the Innovative Links between Schools and Universities Project for Teacher Professional Development. (These projects are described in Chapter 6.) Importantly, in different ways these projects seized two contemporary principles of organizational development: networking and a learning organization approach to change and development. Both were concerned with raising questions and issues that confront what it means to be a teacher, an academic, a policy activist, and how to deal with the complexities, dilemmas and tensions of contemporary educational life. At the core of both of these projects was a commitment to improve the work practices and conditions of teachers and students, and in so doing to improve student learning outcomes.

Rethinking the practice of teacher professionalism requires that all of those involved in education negotiate and renegotiate meanings and processes in order to engage teachers in the broad project of teacher professionalism. As a result of these interactions, professional communities emerge, either as a result of a deliberate strategy to establish them or in response to emerging conditions. The purpose of these communities is the production of shared communal resources, which include routines, sensibilities, artefacts, vocabulary, styles, knowledge etc. that members have developed over time. These develop around things that matter to people, and as such their practices reflect those things that matter to the group (Wenger 1998). For teachers in schools, identification of these varies depending upon the setting, size and type of school (primary/secondary; state/private) as well as the personal histories of the teachers themselves. Nevertheless, these communities are important arenas where teachers might work collaboratively, debate issues and share expertise regarding their practice. Furthermore, structurally and practically they help to remove the sense of isolation that many teachers experience in their daily work in schools. Such communities of practice also provide opportunities to reduce levels of the individualism and conservatism that some scholars argue characterize contemporary schools (see Lortie 1975; A. Hargreaves 1994). These professional communities are informed by various educational discourses which shape not only the form and content of the communities themselves but, more importantly, the debates and practices that occur within them.

Dominant discourses of teacher professionalism

Discourses offer particular kinds of subject positions and identity through which people come to view their relationships with different loci of power (Clarke and Newman 1997: 92). This is an important point given the emergence of two distinct but not entirely oppositional discourses that are dominating educational policies around teacher professionalism. An examination of Australian policy documents at the federal and state levels and public debates in the media reveals that two versions of teacher professionalism are circulating: managerial professionalism and democratic professionalism (Preston 1996). These discourses set the limits of what can be said, thought and done with respect to debates and initiatives which are designed to enhance the political project of teacher professionalism nationally across both state and independent schooling sectors.

Clarke and Newman (1997: 7) suggest that 'professionalism operates as an occupational strategy, defining entry and negotiating the power and rewards due to expertise, and as an organizational strategy, shaping the patterns of power, place and relationships around which organizations are coordinated'. This observation well describes the development of ideologies and policies of teacher professionalism in Australia. The discourses that are currently dominating debates around issues of teacher professionalism assert particular realities and priorities. Sinclair (1995: 232) claims that:

> How people locate themselves in relation to certain discourses reflects the socially sanctioned dominance of certain ideologies and subjugation of others. Because discourses vary in their authority . . . at one particular time one discourse, such as managerialism or market approach, seems 'natural' while another . . . struggles to find expression in the way experience is described.

Indeed, definitions of professionalism, what constitutes a profession and so on have been sites of academic and ideological struggle between union leaders, bureaucrats and academics played out in a variety of settings. It could be said that these diverse groups share no singular version of what constitutes professionalism or teaching as a profession. This is despite the fact that each of these groups claims to be acting in the best interests of teachers individually and collectively.

Recent reform agendas in Australia, the UK and elsewhere have served to challenge traditional conceptions of teacher professionalism and, in particular, issues of teacher autonomy. However, Furlong *et al.* (2000), referring to the UK, argue that the aspiration to change teacher professionalism by influencing the nature of the knowledge, skills and values to which new teachers are exposed is also significant. They go on to argue that 'the assumption behind policy within this area has been that changes in the form and content of initial teacher education will, in the long run, serve to construct a new generation of teachers with different forms of knowledge, different skills and different professional values' (Furlong *et al.* 2000: 6). Recent policies have given rise to a new professionalism among teachers. Significantly, as Furlong *et al.* claim, the time has now long gone when isolated, unaccountable professionals made curriculum and pedagogical decisions alone without reference to the outside world. The new professionalism currently developing, informing various policy documents and now mandated by the state, is what I describe as managerial professionalism. Its attributes, intensions and purposes are elaborated below.

Managerial professionalism

In some respects the discourse of managerial professionalism has been the more dominant of the two discourses given its impact on the work of teachers. This is particularly the case with the consequences of reform initiatives such as organizational change, imperatives for teachers in schools to be more accountable and for systems to be more efficient and economic in their activities. Clarke (1995) suggests that two themes underpin the new managerialism: universalism and isomorphism. Universalism holds that all

organizations are basically the same and, irrespective of their specific functions, need to pursue efficiency. Isomorphism is the assumption that commercial organizations are the most naturally occurring form of coordination,
compared with which public sector organizations are deviant (quoted in
Whitty *et al.* 1998: 52).

In line with broader new public management imperatives, managerial
discourses make two distinct claims: that efficient management can solve
any problem; and that practices which are appropriate for the conduct of
private sector enterprises can also be applied to the public sector (Rees
1995). Furthermore, as Pollitt (1990) notes, the values of managerialism
have been promoted as being universal: management is inherently good,
managers are the heroes, managers should be given the room and autonomy
to manage and other groups should accept their authority. These ideologies
have found themselves to be prevalent in education bureaucracies as well
as in schools themselves, especially in the management practices found in
schools.

Within the education sector, recent policies promoting devolution and
decentralization have provided sympathetic conditions for a discourse of
managerialism to emerge and flourish. One of the consequences of this is
the development of an alternative form of teacher professionalism, one that
gains its legitimacy though the promulgation of policies and the allocation
of funds associated with those policies. I refer to this form of professionalism as managerial professionalism. The new discourse attempts to redefine
what is meant by teacher professionalism and how teachers practise it
individually and collectively. Whitty *et al.* (1998: 65) describe the current
situation well in the UK and elsewhere when they observe:

> Whether or not what we are witnessing here is a struggle between a
> professionalizing project or a deprofessionalizing one, it is certainly a
> struggle among different stakeholders over the definition of teacher
> professionalism and professionality for the twenty-first century.

Where devolution and decentralization have been at the core of reform
agendas teachers are placed in a long line of authority in terms of their
accountability for reaching measurable outcomes that stretches through the
principal, to the district/regional office, to the central office. For Brennan
(1996: 22), this corporate management model emphasizes:

> [a] professional who clearly meets corporate goals, set elsewhere,
> manages a range of students well and documents their achievements
> and problems for public accountability purposes. The criteria of the
> successful professional in this corporate model is of one who works
> efficiently and effectively in meeting the standardized criteria set for
> the accomplishment of both students and teachers, as well as contrib-
> uting to the school's formal accountability processes.

Managerialism has also had a significant impact on the work of school principals as well as on teachers. Recent restructuring has meant that the principal has moved from the role of senior colleague to one of institutional manager. Fergusson (1994: 106) describes the impact of these reforms on the teaching profession:

> [The] reform movement and the drive towards managerialism prudently took the initial professional formation of teachers within its ambit. Together they have led to a careful scrutiny of the sources of notions of professionalism and collective self-concept, and the values, assumptions and expectations that are associated with them: the entire gamut of the processes of group socialization, combined with the development of professional identity and allegiance to academic community.

The new discourses of managerialism offer new subject positions and patterns of identification – those of management as opposed to professionalism. Clarke and Newman (1997: 93) suggest that 'managerial discourses create the possibilities within which individuals construct new roles and identities and from which they derive ideas about the logic of institutional change'. In terms of teachers' professional development and the profession's moves to establish new and more active notions of teacher professionalism, the managerialist approach directly contrasts with democratic professionalism. Furthermore, advocates of each of these kinds of professionalism are often at loggerheads because unions and other professional bodies champion democratic professionalism whereas systems and employers advocate managerial professionalism.

Democratic professionalism

The second of the discourses circulating about teacher professionalism is that of democratic professionalism. Apple (1996) suggests that an alternative to state control is not traditional professionalism, but a democratic professionalism which seeks to demystify professional work and build alliances between teachers and excluded constituencies of students, parts and members of the community on whose behalf decisions have traditionally been made either by professions or by the state.

Preston (1996) argues that democratic professionalism was a concept used by the then Australian Teachers Union (ATU):

> [Democratic professionalism] does not seek to mystify professional work, or to unreasonably restrict access to that work; it facilitates the participation in decision making by students, parents and others and seeks to develop a broader understanding in the community of education and how it operates. As professionals, teachers must be responsible and

accountable for that which is under their control, both individually
and collectively through their unions.

(Australian Teachers Union 1991, quoted in Preston 1996: 192)

The core of democratic professionalism is an emphasis on collaborative,
cooperative action between teachers and other educational stakeholders.
Preston (1996) maintains that this approach is a strategy for industry development, skill development and work organization. It suggests that the teacher
has a wider responsibility than the single classroom and includes contributing to the school, the system, other students, the wider community and
collective responsibilities of teachers themselves as a group and the broader
profession (Brennan 1996).

There have been various attempts in Australia and elsewhere to enhance
teacher professionalism. The National Schools Network (NSN) and Innovative Links project in Australia, the coalition of Essential Schools in the
USA and the Teachers' Network in Singapore are all premised on a democratic view of teacher professionalism. These major initiatives are described
in more detail in Chapter 6. All of these projects do much more than help
teachers develop better ways of improving their practice. Preston (1996),
referring to the NSN in particular, suggests that these projects are developing
and testing better ways of carrying out research to consolidate the knowledge base of the teaching profession through close collaboration between
practising teachers and academics. Through facilitated research, academics
and school-based practitioners work collaboratively in mutually identified
projects. Their focus, their modes of affiliation, forms of documentation
and communication become the vehicle for a more inclusive form of teacher
professionalism. At the core of these activities are new forms of reciprocity
between teachers and academics and other education stakeholders whereby
both groups come to understand the nature and limitations of each other's
work and perspectives.

Teacher professionalism: a struggle for meaning

In Chapter 1, I identified the complexity and the lack of agreement regarding definitions of professionalism. Renewing teacher professionalism means
moving beyond what Freidson (1994) calls a commonsense idea of professionalism, that is one developed passively and which is not elaborated,
systematized or refined self-consciously but rather grows out of everyday
social use. For Freidson (1994: 170):

commonsense usage is expanded to emphasise those characteristics of
an occupation that justify special standing and privilege: it becomes a

profession's portrayal of profession. Its content is determined largely by the political and ceremonial needs of the profession, and it is used primarily to advance and defend its position.

Through award restructuring and the various teacher professional development initiatives that emerged during the 1990s in response to federal government support, teacher professionalism in Australia developed beyond Freidson's commonsense view. It became a vehicle for school reform and the political repositioning of the profession both in terms of itself but more importantly in the eyes of the community. It became a vehicle for developing new kinds of professional affiliation and activity. As a consequence, teacher learning became increasingly important.

One of the hallmarks of being identified externally as a professional is to continue learning throughout a career, deepening knowledge, skill judgement, staying abreast of important developments in the field and experimenting with innovations that promise improvements in practice (Sykes 1990). Here lies one of the paradoxes for teacher professionalism, for as Fullan (1993) notes, as a profession, we are not a learning profession. Whereas student learning is a goal, the continuing learning of teachers is often overlooked. Whereas continuous learning and the improvement of teaching practice should be one of the core values of teacher professionalism, in many instances this is not so.

The type of systemic school reform that has characterized recent education policy and practices has established new sets of relations among governmental bureaucracies and agencies, unions, professional teaching groups in both primary and secondary areas, and research communities. The call for teacher professionalism, through award restructuring and school reform, is also related to a revision of occupational identity. Paradoxically, it gave value to school work that included greater teacher responsibility and flexibility in implementing state policy. Under the guise of professionalism, teachers became the vehicles to implement government policy, which had as its central priority increased productivity by being more efficient, effective and economic in all aspects of practice.

The work identity promoted through national teacher professional development initiatives and some aspects of the more general educational reform agenda in Australia recast teachers as learners and researchers. School-based national projects which break with traditional parochial conceptions of teacher professionalism have been implemented in various countries. They have been successful because teachers participate as part of a national network of teachers involved in professional development, whereby they become part of the national reform agenda, and are inclusive of a national professional group. Indeed, the national nature of such projects has created a vigorous professional community within schools and across system and state boundaries which has given life to the development of new ideas and practices which move well beyond local needs and interests.

In Australia, both the NSN and the Innovative Links project attempted to broaden the base of school restructuring beyond organizational change to incorporate the view of the need to rethink the practice of teacher professionalism. The aim was to bring about significant changes in teacher practices which, it was argued, would then improve student learning outcomes. The NSN and Innovative Links project have provided the vehicle whereby organizations might legitimately be restructured so that good ideas and strategies born in practice can flourish and not be hindered by existing bureaucratic forces (Grimmet 1995).

The NSN and Innovative Links project have shown the significance of developing a national approach to the renewal of teacher professionalism in several respects. First, it provided teachers with opportunities to cross over state and system boundaries to access information and best practice that is of professional value. They facilitated networking of the kind that is different from the traditional cross-local-school type. It broke teachers out of their local systems, and thus broke them out of the parochialism of that system, and attached their sense of professional identity to a wider, more open and comparative system orientation. Second, the use of national forums as a strategy for bringing project participants together not only enabled the 'big picture' of school reform and teacher professionalism to be presented, but also supported the development of national networks. Third, the presence of the university as part of a reform site known as a roundtable contributed to the national character of the project. In Australia, universities, unlike schools, are federally funded. Teacher education academics identify as members of a national professional group, and see their professional networks as national and international rather than as state or local in nature (Yeatman and Sachs 1995). Finally, these projects contributed in constructive ways to making real the possibility of revitalized teaching in revitalized schools (Grimmett 1995).

A platform for rethinking the practice of teacher professionalism

A new form of teacher professionalism requires a different framework by which to think about and mobilize the teaching profession. Drawing on the experience of the NSN and Innovative Links project, I suggest that there are five elements that contribute to this: learning, participation, collaboration, cooperation and activism. Taken together these specify what it means to be a socially responsible and active professional for the new millennium.

They constitute the fundamentals of a proactive and responsible approach to teacher professionalism.

1 Learning

Learning is at the core of rethinking teacher professionalism. As an individual and collective goal, teachers should be seen to practise the value of learning, both with their colleagues and with their students. By recasting themselves as learners, the social relations of schools and the relations between teachers and teachers, teachers and students, and teachers and their communities, will be fundamentally reshaped. Learning rather than teaching becomes the core activity of teacher and student life in schools. For some teachers this will require a significant shift in how they organize their work, and how they see themselves as teachers. For some it will provide a much-needed injection of life into routinized and ritualized behaviours in their classrooms.

As teachers are one of the many resources in schools, their own learning must be fostered. Day (1999: 2) maintains that:

> They stand at the interface of the transmission of knowledge, skills and values. Teachers will only be able to fulfil their educational purposes if they are both well prepared for the profession and able to maintain and improve their contribution to it through life-long learning.

Regarding the significance of learning in personal transformation, Wenger (1998: 215) makes the important point that:

> Because learning transforms who we are and what we can do, it is an experience of identity. It is not just an accumulation of skills and information, but also a process of becoming – to become a certain person, or conversely, to avoid becoming a certain person.

Learning, then, for teachers has personal, professional and political dimensions. The personal relates to their own growth and understanding of the world about them; the professional requires that they continue to develop skills, content and competencies as these relate to their own areas of expertise; the political is in the sense that an informed and educated teaching force will be able to mount compelling arguments for and against the implementation of some policies that may or may not be in the best interests of students and other stakeholders.

2 Participation

Recasting the social relationship of schooling demands active participation by teachers, students and their communities. It requires shifts in how institutions are organized, which in turn affects how people relate to each other. At the organizational level, new structures need to be put in place so that all members of an education community have opportunities to contribute to debates about policy and practice. Here the expertise of various groups is utilized with the result that new insights and strategies may emerge that may previously not have been considered. This strategy requires the development of trust across all constituencies, and as Fullan and Hargreaves (1992) assert, it is trust in people and processes. Accordingly, risk is rewarded in such contexts, with new solutions to recurring problems being a positive outcome.

Reclaiming teacher professionalism through participation requires that teachers see themselves as active agents in their own professional worlds. This can happen only if they are encouraged to be active and if structures are developed which tap and enhance their agency (Yeatman 1996a). A participative approach to teacher professionalism cannot go very far unless it is adopted and agreed upon as a core value and strategies are put in place to develop and support it by all those involved in the education enterprise.

3   Collaboration

Collaboration has two main dimensions: internal and external. Internally, collaboration, collegiality and conversation provide teachers with a means for professional learning and development within the context of self and community (Beattie 1995). Coming together as collaborative groups or teams allows for a synergy that would not otherwise be possible. Team-based or collaboratively oriented conversation enables the kind of dialogue through which people as individuals and as a group change what they think and, possibly, feel about something or someone (Yeatman 1996a).

Externally, collaboration involves working with other interested parties outside of the school locale. This could include community groups, or academics working in universities. These partnerships provide opportunities for new kinds of expertise to be developed on the part of both school-based personnel and their university-based colleagues, as well as by members of the broader community.

Collaboration and cooperation are terms that are often used interchangeably. However for our purposes it is important to differentiate between the two. Collaboration involves joint decision-making, requires time, careful negotiation, trust and effective communication – all parties are learners in which the outcome is improved professional dialogue. For cooperation, role boundaries and power are left unquestioned and reinforced through formal and informal structures. There is little mutual learning in what is in essence an expert–client type of relationship, where the benefits are more one way, that is, in the interests of those who have most to gain.

4   Cooperation

Historically, teachers have had limited opportunities to work with their peers in collaborative and cooperative ways. There is little tradition in the teaching profession of learning from each other and developing expertise collectively in written or oral form. As a profession, teachers have developed neither a common language nor a technology for documenting and discussing practice and its outcomes. This is partly owing to the pragmatic nature of teaching itself, the conditions under which teachers work, the precedents set by practice, the intangibility of its consequences, and the intensity and immediacy of the work of teaching. Collectively these factors reinforce a professional dialogue in which spoken rather than written language is the more highly valued and practised mode of communication, and which more often than not comprises immediate responses rather than considered reflection on practice. Furthermore, it reinforces a practical orientation to the discussion and solution of educational issues and problems.

Cooperating with peers by rethinking work practices along cooperative lines helps to break down individualism and isolationism. Furthermore, it facilitates a mode of working where trust can be engendered and new solutions to recurrent problems can be debated and trialled. Again, learning becomes central to a teacher's work, as does improving practice that results from that learning.

5   Activism

Being active means engaging with and responding to issues that relate directly or indirectly to education and schooling. It involves participation, collaboration and cooperation from within and outside the profession. It means standing up for what Fullan (1993) describes as the moral purpose of teaching. It also requires that others are involved individually and collectively as change agents Fullan (1993). On the role of the individual teacher it is worth quoting Fullan at length:

> The individual educator is a critical starting point because the leverage of change can be greater through the efforts of individuals, and each educator has some control (more than is exercised) over what he or she does, because it is one's own motives and skills that are at question.
>
> (Fullan 1993: 12)

This type of activism is intellectually and politically demanding. It requires risk-taking and fighting for ideals that will enhance education. It also requires passion, determination and energy. Not surprisingly, activism is probably safer as a collective activity than as an individual one. Nevertheless, individual action has its place, and sometimes individual ideas are generated and then taken up by a larger group. The idea of the activist teacher profession is developed in more detail in the last chapter.

These five principles for rethinking the practice of teacher professionalism – learning, participation, collaboration, cooperation and activism – together form a platform upon which teacher professionalism can be renewed and developed. Taken in isolation, any one of these values does not contribute to the overall project of rethinking teacher professionalism. Alternatively, when viewed in conjunction with the other values, each becomes powerful and effective in its overall professional and political effect. These values should stand at the core of building a socially and politically responsible profession. Following Hargreaves and Goodson (1996: 20), renewing teacher professionalism to incorporate the above values is a 'struggle which is guided by moral and political visions of the purposes which teacher professionalism should serve within actively caring communities and vigorous social democracies'. It is an activity that is worth intellectual and emotional investment.

Successful projects that have aimed at revitalizing teacher professionalism represent examples of postmodern professionalism (Goodson and Hargreaves 1996). They provide examples of what is possible when teachers reclaim the professional agenda. These projects, individually and collectively, have been guided by a shared vision of the purposes which teacher professionalism should serve within active social and political communities. Like Hargreaves and Goodson's (1996: 20–1) attributes of teacher professionalism in a complex, postmodern age, schools involved with initiatives to reclaim the agenda for teacher professionalism have:

1 increased opportunity and responsibility to exercise *discretionary judgement* over issues of teaching, curriculum and the care that affects one's students;
2 opportunities and expectations to engage with the *moral and social purposes and value* of what teachers teach, along with major curriculum and assessment matters in which these purposes are embedded;
3 commitment to working with colleagues in *collaborative cultures* of help and support as ways of using shared expertise to solve ongoing problems of professional practice, rather than engaging in joint work as a motivational device to implement external mandates of others;
4 a self-directed search and struggle for *continuous learning* related to one's own expertise and standards of practice, rather than compliance with the enervating obligations of endless change demanded by others (often under the guise of continuous learning or improvement).

A fifth attribute might be added to this condensed list, namely that such schools can:

5 become part of a national social movement in which teachers individually and collectively develop skills, competencies and dispositions of mind that will contribute to the enhancement of teaching and the improvement of student learning outcomes.

School-based and national projects by their conception, organization and membership have provided teachers with opportunities to take an active role in defining their own professional needs and how these needs might be achieved. These projects have recast relationships between a variety of education workers and have contributed to providing models for how teachers can be responsible both for their own learning and for improving that of students. That these projects transcend state boundaries and confront the conventional wisdom of experience is in no small part due to the vision and commitment of a number of teachers, academic and policy activists working at state and national levels. Their energy and strategic thinking have played an important part in the project of reclaiming teacher professionalism in Australia. However, in the end, it is teachers themselves who have the responsibility of sustaining and reclaiming the professional agenda.

Conclusion

In this chapter I have described the general features of public sector management reform that provided the conditions for major educational reform initiatives in Australia, the UK and elsewhere. The new public sector reform agenda gave rise to a variety of education discourses that informed education policy and teacher practice. In Australia in particular, new forms of association were developed between federal and state governments, unions and employing authorities which were enshrined in the Teaching Accord. While this Accord is no longer operational, its legacy is evident, especially its project to enhance teacher professionalism. The fact that two national projects were spawned from the Accord speaks of its vision and conceptual power. That there are residual effects evident in the work practices of teachers further underscores its importance.

Current education policies have given rise to two forms of teacher professionalism: managerial and democratic professionalism. While these two forms of teacher professionalism seem to be at either end of the spectrum, teachers' identification with them and how they impact on their work is not so oppositional. Teachers are likely to identify with either or both depending on the contexts in which they are working.

Finally, I have developed a platform for rethinking teacher professionalism founded upon five principles: learning, participation, collaboration, cooperation and activism. To operationalize an alternative form of teacher professionalism is no easy matter, especially when governments and employing authorities would prefer to have a compliant teaching profession. Nevertheless, when teachers work collectively with various stakeholders the promise of a revitalized teaching profession becomes a possibility.

Note

1 The AEU is the national union representing teachers working in state schools, whereas the IEU represents at the national level teachers working in independent and Catholic schools.

three

The politics of teacher professionalism

The idea of standards for the teaching profession has been circulating in education policy discourses and debates for much of the latter part of the 1990s. The ownership of the development and content of such standards should be part of the political project of teacher professionalism. This project involves developing a considered strategy that moves beyond the immediate needs of professional self-interest. Furthermore, it requires an acknowledgement that inherent within current debates about teacher professionalism and teacher professional standards is the contradiction of the competing discourses and practices that revolve around professional self-interest versus professional control and ownership. Leadership in the field of professional standards will require a deft touch that balances these competing discourses and their associated practices.

The development of standards has been part of a two-pronged initiative by governments and bureaucracies in Australia, the UK, USA and elsewhere to improve the educational performance and outcomes of education systems and the practices of teachers in classrooms. Debates and initiatives regarding teacher professional standards have been concerned with two orientations: the use of standards to improve performance or the use of standards as a basis for reforming the teaching profession. In applying these orientations to professional standards, in some settings these standards have been imposed by governments and used as regulatory frameworks and bureaucratic controls over teachers, particularly as they relate to licensing and certification procedures. In other instances they are used as an initiative for teachers to gain professional control over what constitutes professional work. Darling Hammond (1999: 39), writing from a North American perspective, argues: 'Recently developed professional standards for teaching hold promise for mobilizing reforms of the teaching career and helping to structure the learning opportunities that reflect the complex, reciprocal nature of teaching work'. In terms of current initiatives, there are two sets of tensions present. The first concerns where the initiative to develop the standards comes from and how the standards are monitored. On the one hand there are those standards developed and imposed by state-mandated regulatory bodies outside of the profession, and on the other hand there are those developed and monitored by the profession itself. Either way, the issue of standards is neither straightforward nor unproblematical to the teaching profession. A second, but no less important, tension is that there is a tendency to focus on standardization of practice rather the development of standards that can have wide applicability across various contexts and settings or even of improving the level of standards achieved.

Mahony and Hextall (2000: 31) differentiate between regulatory and developmental approaches to standards. Regulatory approaches can be used as a managerialist tool for measuring the efficiency and effectiveness of systems, institutions and individuals. Developmental approaches, on the other hand, provide opportunities for teachers' further professional learning, aimed at improving the quality of their teaching throughout their careers.

Although in the UK, Australia and USA both of these approaches to standards are evident, there is an emerging trend for a drift from developmental to regulatory approaches to standards. In the UK, for example, the development of the national professional standards (NPS) can be seen both as providing a centralized specification of 'effective teaching' and as the codification of relations between managers and managed (Mahony and Hextall 2000: 32).

In the UK between 1994 and 1998, the Teacher Training Agency (TTA) developed a framework of national standards for teaching, which would 'define expertise in key roles' (TTA 1998: 1). Furlong *et al.* (2000) claim that policies in the late 1990s sought to exploit the new control system by beginning to specify the content of professional education in detail. They claim that 'two strategies were involved: first the transformation of competencies into more elaborate "standards"; second the development of a national curriculum for initial teacher education in English, mathematics, science and information and communication technology' (Furlong *et al.* 2000: 149–50).

In the UK, the move to standards emerged from the competencies debates. This move was to define the content of training in much more explicit detail than before. As the circular stated, 'the standards have been written to be specific, explicit and assessable and are designed to provide a clear basis for the reliable and consistent award of Qualified Teachers Status (QTS), (DfEE 1997: 6). Millett (1997) suggests that the standards for the award of Qualified Teachers Status set out in more detail than ever before the core knowledge, understandings and skills on which effective teaching rests. These standards replace more 'general "competencies" which had been in force previously and apply to all those assessed for QTS no matter what initial training course or route to teaching they may be on' (quoted in Furlong *et al.* 2000: 150).

An uncritical gaze would suggest that standards are in the best interests of teachers, students and the teaching profession, and indeed this may well be the case. However, the need to be cautious about the limitations of standards is expressed by Darling Hammond (1999: 39):

> Teaching standards are not a magic bullet. By themselves, they cannot solve the problems of dysfunctional school organizations, outmoded curricula, inequitable allocation of resources, or lack of social supports for children and youth. Standards, like all reforms, hold their own dangers. Standard setting in all professions must be vigilant against the possibilities that practice could become constrained by the codification of knowledge that does not significantly acknowledge legitimate diversity of approaches or advances in the field; that access to practice could become overly restricted on grounds not directly related to competence; or that adequate learning opportunities for candidates to meet standards may not emerge on an equitable basis.

In this chapter, I argue that we need to look critically at the issue of professional standards for teachers and the claims that are made by their advocates. In particular, we need to ask whose interests are served by these standards and what are the effects of their imposition on teachers individually and collectively. Finally, we need to ask whether the standards judged as appropriate for today's teaching conditions and teachers will be equally appropriate in the future. Standards cannot and should not be frozen in time; they must be flexible to the changing conditions of teaching and learning as these activities occur inside and outside of schools.

The examination of standards is not a simple or straightforward matter. It is worth quoting Mahony and Hextall (2000) at length to appreciate the complexity of the task.

> In examining standards it is important to examine them for their clarity, consistency and coherence, as well as the values, principles and assumptions that underpin them. They also need to be examined in terms of fitness of purpose – are they capable of doing the work they are intended to do? And is this consistent with the broader purposes of their institutional setting? Procedurally, standards can be investigated in terms of their establishment and formation, with all the questions of accountability and transparency that this entails. They can also be

questioned in terms of the manner in which they are translated into practice and the consequences, both manifest and latent, which follow. More broadly, there is a set of issues to consider in relation to the culture and ideology of standards as a widespread phenomenon operating across both the private and public sectors in England and elsewhere.

Those advocating the advantages of implementing standards regimes make various claims. Three such are: (1) the introduction of standards should improve the performance of teachers (Ingvarson 1998a,b,c); (2) the introduction of standards will improve the standing of teachers (Chadbourne 1999), and (3) standards contribute to the ongoing professional learning of teachers (Ingvarson 1998a,b,c, 1999).

It is clear that the issue of standards has both political and professional dimensions. In the UK the change of language from 'competencies' to 'standards' represented both of these dimensions. Rather than the notion of a minimum ability as implied in the word 'competence', the idea of standards of professional training crossed easily into government concerns to raise educational standards more generally. As such, the change in term had political advantages, making enforcement even more difficult to resist. After all, asked Furlong *et al.* (2000: 151), who could be opposed to raising standards?

Professional teaching standards: what do we mean?

The phrase 'professional teaching standards' is widely and uncritically used in educational policy documents and popular discourses. For Andrew (1997: 168):

> in this era of standards, writers use the term in many different ways, seldom bothering to unpack the differences in meaning; standards become the answer to all questions. They are thought to provide the magic ingredient to restructuring all education.

The language of standards, then, is important, and as indicated in the UK, the move from competencies to standards had obvious political attractions. The language and the content of the standards indicate the purpose to which the standards will be applied. I suggest that four versions of standards are circulating in current policy debates and documents, and that they focus on measuring the performance of teachers, to improving or developing the teaching profession. These are standards as common sense, standards for quality assurance, standards for quality improvement and standards for certification and control. The more managerial and externally mandated the standards, the more developed are the techniques for measuring the outcomes of teacher performance and the more likely it is that they are used to control teacher professionalism. At the other end of the scale are the standards that have a developmental intent and which signal a more democratic form of teacher professionalism.

Standards as common sense

At present in Australia and elsewhere there appear to be several versions or orientations circulating regarding the meaning of the word 'standards'. The first is a commonsense one, where standards supply the basis for providing a benchmark of what are minimum levels of achievement in various aspects of teaching practice. Standards thus define what teachers should be able to do and what they should know. This version is found in media reports claiming the decline of public education, the decline of standards and so on. It is purely normative in its intent and orientation. The purpose of a commonsense view of teacher professional standards is to present an uncritical view of professional standards, in other words that it makes sense to put in place a regulatory framework that provides for 'quality'. Alternatively, I suggest that the purpose of this view is to promote the use and development of standards as a mechanism to control teachers and the teaching profession. This position sees the application of bureaucratic forces such as rules, mandates and requirements as a means to provide direct supervision, standardized work processes or standardized outcomes to control or regulate teaching (Sergiovani 1998). Indeed, what might be seen to be common sense here has significant implications for teacher autonomy and teacher professionalism.

Apple (2001: 84) claims that:

> a set of national or state standards, national or state curricular, and national or state tests would provide the conditions for thick morality. After all, such regulatory reforms are supposedly based on shared values and common sentiments that also create social spaces in which common issues of concern can be debated and made subject to moral interrogation. Yet what counts as 'common' and how and by whom it is actually determined, is rather more thin than thick.

Clearly, then, commonsense versions of standards are problematical. While sometimes there is an element of good sense in them, more often than not complex issues are simplified and reduced to meaningless cant. Commonsense versions of standards obviously have attractions for political advocates of standards and, all to often, as Apple pointed out, the assumptions of what are common may not be common among various constituencies.

Standards for quality assurance

The second usage, sometimes derived from the first mentioned above, is in terms of public accountability. In is clearly in line with the regulatory approach identified by Mahony and Hextall (2000) above. In Australia, a preference for a regulatory approach is evident in the Senate Inquiry into the Teaching Profession, *A Class Act* (1998). Here standards are seen as:

> essentially concerned with quality assurance and accountability. Quality assurance is generally understood as the process by which users (but also producers) of a service or product can be confident of its consistency, reliability, safety and to some extent its 'value for money'. Such assurances are normally predicated on certain key assumptions about the conditions under which the product or service will be used, and the nature of the users involved.
>
> Accountability involves the requirement that one group (here a profession) provide an account or justification of its activities to another group in return for the trust or privileges granted to the former by the latter. Accountability also normally involves the expectation that the accountable group be willing to accept advice or criticism from the public and to modify its practices in the light of that advice or criticism.
>
> (Senate Employment, Education and Training Reference Committee 1998: 12)

This definition of standards denotes a degree of quality or an assessment of quality. It has clear emotional/evaluative connotations. The intent here can be seen to be political, in that the implicit and explicit aim is to elevate the status of the teaching profession in the eyes of the general public and other professions. Of course, who sets the standards and how they are set becomes one of the sites of struggle between the profession and other stakeholders, and indeed, more often than not, it is omitted from the discourse. Whether or not this omission is intentional is unclear but it certainly has very clear effects, both in terms of the nature of the debate and also in terms of its outcomes, especially the autonomy of the teaching profession.

In the UK, standards for the award of the QTS were premised regulatory assumptions. Mahony and Hextall (2000: 34) argue that they were regulatory in two ways. First, within a context where a variety of routes into teaching have been actively encouraged, QTS standards claim to provide a quality assurance mechanism in relation to individuals entering teaching. Second, the standards relate to the institutions providing initial teacher training (ITT). The question of whether ITT providers enable trainees to meet the standards forms the basis on which they are inspected by Ofsted.

The list of standards developed in the UK was not new; it was simply a development of earlier lists – an amalgam of historical precedent moderated by current political demands. As Atkinson and Claxton (1999) point out, the form of presentation gave little insight into the nature and quality of teaching – how it is fundamentally related to aims and goals; how skills, knowledge and understandings are interrelated and in part intuitive. Nor do the standards acknowledge the importance of context in the measurement of teaching performance and student learning outcomes.

Standards for quality improvement

A third orientation, unlike the quality assurance perspective, is one based on a notion of quality improvement; this is a developmental approach to standards mentioned earlier. Ingvarson (1998a,b,c) and Darling Hammond (1998) both promote this view in the context of teachers' professional development, learning and career advancement. For Ingvarson (1998c: 1016), 'Professional standards can be seen as an attempt to conceptualize the main dimensions along which teachers can be expected to improve their practice'. Furthermore, 'professional development planning driven by standards – whether they be standards for initial registration, appraisal or promotion, looks to the long term. It focuses on teachers as persons, where they are and what they might become, not just the present policy change' (1998c: 1027). Similarly, Darling Hammond (1998) suggests that current initiatives to establish standards reflect the growing knowledge base about teaching and a growing consensus about what teachers should know and be able to do in order to help students learn.

The making explicit of norms of professional conduct and practice to which pupils ought to be entitled and of which a wider public has a legitimate right to be assured is of central importance in the quality improvement or developmental approach to standards (Mahony and Hextall 2000: 31). The publication of norms of professional conduct and practice make for transparency regarding the social and professional expectations and obligations of teachers. This obviates possibilities emerging of unwarranted criticism by external groups because of ambiguity and uncertainty of intent or meaning. These kinds of standards are most likely to be in the best interests of teaching, especially the development of a strong and autonomous teaching profession.

Standards, certification or control

The phrase 'professional standards' is sometimes used interchangeably with professional certification and licensing. Following Darling Hammond (1999), 'licensing' is used to describe state decisions about admission to practice and 'certification' is used to describe the actions of professional instrumentalities (such as the National Board for Professional Teaching Standards in the USA) in certifying accomplished practice. For the purposes of this chapter the focus is on certification, in particular how it relates to the development and recognition of the teaching profession. Ingvarson (1999: 68) makes the important point that:

> The power of professional certification depends fundamentally on the credibility of the standards and the rigour of the methods used to assess teacher performance. One of the main aims of certification is to place more value on teachers' work. Without the rigour, the value of the professional recognition is diminished ... certification provides incentives for all teachers to move towards high standards of practice and to ensure their practice is consistent with current research and professional values.

Ingvarson's position is premised on the assumption that members of the teaching profession develop standards themselves. The development of standards by the National Board for Professional Teaching Standards in the USA was done over an extended period by teachers and with cooperation from various teacher representative bodies. In Australia, on the other hand, the development of standards has not had the luxury of time or the political independence evident in the USA. The same can probably be said about the development of standards in the UK. There have been important consequences of this for the development of Australian standards. Louden (1999: 1) suggests that unlike the US standards, Australian standards frameworks have been more quickly developed, more closely aligned to the needs of state education departments, with less involvement of professional associations and other stakeholder groups, with less attention to assessment strategies, and at considerably less expense. Louden claims that because of the way standards were developed, who developed them and their political intent, there is a series of weaknesses common to all Australian standards.

Because standards in Australia and the UK have been set, in the main, by administrative agencies such as Departments of Education and the Teacher Training Agency, they tacitly emphasize bureaucratic rather than professional controls over teaching. These controls are aimed at standardizing procedures rather than building knowledge that can be applied differently depending on the demands of a particular subject, the social context of a particular community, or the needs of a given student (Darling Hammond 1999). These types of standard are more likely than not to take control away from teachers thus reducing their personal autonomy.

Some claims regarding teaching standards

While the original intention of those supporting the introduction of teacher professional standards may been seen to be generous and in the best interests of the teaching profession, some of the claims may well prove to be naive and inadvertently work against the initial project of professionalizing teaching because they cannot be empirically substantiated. In what follows I identify three claims that have public appeal, would seem to be in the best interests of teaching and would enhance the teaching profession. These claims are: (1) the introduction of standards should improve the performance of teachers; (2) the introduction of standards will improve the standing of teachers, and (3) standards contribute to the ongoing learning of teachers.

The introduction of standards should improve the performance of teachers

Advocates of this position base their argument on the premise that standards should be used for determining goals and exemplars of best practice (Andrew 1997). This is good sense if it is to be implemented in a spirit of the best interests of teachers and students with a focus on the improvement of practice. However, in worst case scenarios the application of standards may serve a gatekeeping function. Andrew (1997: 170) cautions us that:

> Overly zealous gatekeepers who gain power over accreditation and licensing may well produce a massive *teach-to-the-test* response that will divert efforts at improving teaching and teacher education, *dumb down* high quality and innovative programs . . .

Ingvarson's (1998a,c, 1999) celebration of Jeanne Snowa's professional learning through National Board for Professional Teaching Standards in Language Arts in the USA provides ample evidence that the process in documenting her professional knowledge and levels of competency did have consequences for student learning. According to Ingvarson (1998a,c: 40), the processes focused Snowa's attention constantly and in unavoidable ways on her own teaching over a long period of time. For Ingvarson, Snowa's experience provides evidence of a link between teacher learning and consequent student learning (Ingvarson 1999: 68–9). This may be so; however, we do have to question the investment of time, the transfer of learning and the appropriateness of generalizing one case across a whole profession. Furthermore, we should not forget that since the establishment of the National Board of Professional Teaching Standards in 1987 very few teachers have invested the time and money needed to gain accreditation. One has to question whether the financial return of only 900 teachers being certified by the National Board is a solid return on a large financial and political investment when the tenets of efficiency, economy and effectiveness are driving other parts of education policy and practice. Paradoxically, these low numbers are despite the fact that in some states of the USA there is financial support and incentives for teachers to do this. Susan Moore Johnson (2000: 24) claims that 'not only is the number of National Board Certified Teachers small, but their distribution across the country is uneven. What, then, is it about the process, its benefits for teachers and the personal investment required that is standing in the way of more teachers gaining accreditation? Furthermore, perhaps more fundamental questions need to be asked about the conditions under which teachers are working, what sustains teachers, what aspects of their professional life need development, and finally, what are the costs? These questions are left silent by the advocates of professional standards.

At a time when education budgets across the board are being reduced, and when there is increasing accountability but with fewer resources to assure quality, the cost of professional development is being carried by teachers themselves, in terms both of financial cost and of investment of time. This is a difficult call. Critics demand that teachers work harder, and identify their 'short' working hours and their 'long' holidays as evidence of their under-deployment in comparison with other occupations. However, the state also has some responsibility in the provision of resources for teachers to develop their knowledge and skills.

Another weakness with this position is that it leaves silent the assumptions about how professional development or accreditation will occur and what model of change will be used to implement it. Sergiovani (1998) suggests that if a bureaucratic or personal change forces perspective is taken, then rules, mandates and requirements will impose regimes of direct supervision and standardized work upon teachers and schools collectively. Alternatively, if schools are seen as communities then professional forces which rely on standards of expertise, codes of conduct, collegiality, felt obligations and other professional norms will be used to build a professional community. Obviously both of these approaches have appeal to different constituencies.

In order for this position to have some currency among teachers and others, some of the assumptions about the nature of the teaching and how to improve it need to be made more explicit. This could be done by creating opportunities for critical debate about the nature of teaching and having the outcomes of such debates circulated around the profession so that they are owned and approved by teachers themselves.

The introduction of standards will improve the standing of teachers

This second claim suggests that the application of standards to the teaching profession will enhance the status of the teaching profession. This was a position favoured by the Australian Senate Inquiry into the Status of Teaching as set out in its report *A Class Act*. For Ingvarson (1998c: 1006), 'In a standards based model, profession-defined standards provide the basis on which the profession can lay down its own agenda and expectations for professional development and accountability'.

The standing of teaching will be developed only if there is strong community support for teachers collectively. For many there is little that is esoteric about teaching: everyone has had experience of it and has an opinion on how to teach and what the attributes of quality teaching are. Their experience of schooling and teachers gives them the evidence to pass judgement.

A public media campaign that promotes 'teacher bashing' and focuses on the few 'incompetent' teachers does little to promote the status of teaching. Declining work conditions, reduced public funding and the politicization of education policy and practice further diminish the standing of teachers in the eyes of the community. It is questionable whether the publication and implementation of professional teaching standards will transform the public's perception of teachers and the value that is placed on teachers. What is required is a sustained campaign in support of public education, a campaign where the accomplishments of teachers are celebrated, where the stories and narratives of teachers are told and the contribution that teachers make to the individual lives of their students and to society collectively are publicized. This requires the emergence of a new kind of teacher professional, one that I call the activist professional (Sachs 2000). Activist professionals work in different ways with their colleagues and other educational stake-holders. They work collectively towards strategic ends; they operate on the basis of developing networks and alliances between bureaucracies, unions, professional associations and community organizations. These alliances are not static; they form and are reformed around different issues and concerns. Activist professionals take responsibility for their own ongoing professional learning, they work within communities of practice which develop in larger contexts – historical, social, cultural, institutional – with specific reference to resources and constraints (Wenger 1998).

I suggest that it is a new identity and changing community perceptions of teachers and experiences of schools that will enhance the status of teaching. It is unlikely that a standards framework will turn around a non-supportive press or embedded community prejudices.

In the UK, the establishment of the General Teaching Council in 2000 also aimed at enhancing the status of teaching. The then Minister for school standards, Stephen Byers, wrote:

We intend to set up a General Teaching Council (GTC) by the year 2000. It will play an important role in raising the status and standing of the teaching profession, and will contribute to our drive to raise standards.

There has long been agreement that a GTC is desirable. It will enhance the standing of teachers by giving them a clear professional voice, independent of government but working with us to raise standards. It will help to restore the morale of teachers, who for too long have had too little say in determining the shape and future of their profession. It will celebrate the best of teaching, by drawing on the dedication and experience of those who have made teaching their vocation. It will be able to promote a positive image of teaching both within the profession and outside.

(DfEE 1997: 3)

Clearly this kind of celebratory rhetoric is welcome but paradoxically it is happening at a time when there is increasing intervention by the state on the types and models of teacher professionalism sanctioned and available to teachers.

Standards contribute to the ongoing professional learning of teachers

As I suggested earlier, Ingvarson is passionate in his support of the application of professional standards for teachers which, he argues, will contribute to the ongoing professional learning of teachers. He advocates a standards-guided professional development system as an alternative to, not a substitute for, traditional models of in-service education (Ingvarson 1998c). According to Ingvarson, 'In the standards-guided model, profession defined standards provide the basis on which the profession can lay down its own agenda and expectations for professional development and accountability' (1998c: 1006).

Ingvarson draws on the National Council for Teaching of Mathematics' *Professional Standards for the Teaching of Mathematics* to develop what he sees as the components of a standards-guided model for the ongoing professional learning of teachers. These are:

1 Profession defined *teaching standards* that provide direction and milestones for professional development over the long term of a career of teaching;
2 An *infrastructure for professional learning* whose primary purpose is to enable teachers to gain the knowledge and skill embodied in the teaching standards;
3 Staged career structures and pay systems that provide *incentives and recognition* for attaining these teaching standards;

4 A credible system of *professional certification* based on valid assessments of whether teachers have attained levels of performance defined by the standards.

(Ingvarson 1998c: 1009, italics in original)

The logic of these is undeniable, as is their good sense for the enhancement of the teaching profession and facilitating the ongoing professional learning of teachers. In particular, 1 and 2 should be seen as the cornerstone of every teacher's professional code of practice. Indeed, work being undertaken in Australia by Ingvarson, Louden and their colleagues in the development of professional standards in mathematics, English and literacy, and science in conjunction with Departments of Education, professional associations and unions, is going some considerable way to putting the first two components of a standards-based model into practice.

In developing the standards themselves, teachers should have control over what is identified as the standard. This in itself is a valuable professional development activity. Given the competing demands on teachers personally and professionally, the issue to be addressed is, should these activities be mandatory or should groups of teachers at various stages of their careers be identified as possible targets? Indeed, which teachers are likely to gain the most benefit? Day (1999) suggests that teachers who, in Huberman's terms, have reached a professional plateau, may seek opportunities 'to re-examine the basis upon which their assumptions and beliefs about teaching are founded, question the purposes and contexts of their work, review and renew their intellectual commitments through further study either by participating in school, local education authority or district networks or participating in further degree work' (Day 1999: 62). This group may well be one with which to begin. The question still needs to be asked, will teachers collectively and individually see these as priorities and not simply as extra work at a time when their workloads are being intensified and new curricula are being implemented? While ongoing professional learning should be seen as a fundamental part of teachers' work, many teachers are, like some of their students, reluctant learners. Given the small take-up of National Board Teacher Certification in the USA, the issue of teacher professional learning credentials is one that needs to be taken up by unions and bureaucracies and at the same time supported financially by governments whatever their persuasion.

Components 3 and 4 are more difficult for the profession to control or influence. They are the most political dimension of a standards schema. These two components circulate around a number of professional and industrial issues. They are professional because teachers' professional knowledge, expertise and competency are codified and made public, and industrial because these issues have implications about the working conditions, recognition and rewarding of teacher learning. Successful negotiation of career structures and pay scales require an Accord between unions, employers and government. In Australia, the demise of the Teaching Accord developed in the early 1990s does not auger well for such an activity, nor does the failure of the Advanced Skills Teacher designation to be embedded in industrial or professional contracts mean that these components will be easily put in place. These components speak of the political aspects of standards and their acceptance by governments, employing authorities and unions alike, not to mention teachers themselves.

The implementation of teaching standards does have implications for teachers' work. Any failure to acknowledge this is naive. Menter *et al.* (1997: 132) note:

> It is worth remembering that constant reworking of strategies for the control of teachers' work develops in response to the independent actions of teachers themselves, as well as in consequence of the contradictory functions of education systems. So teachers are not the mere recipients of policy, nor are they understood as endlessly manipulable . . . they have strong work cultures and considerable loyalty and dedication to the education service. . . . [This] is at once a source of strength and a characteristic which renders them vulnerable to exploitation.

As a note of caution: while, in the eyes of its advocates, teacher professional standards may well enhance the status of teachers and contribute to the ongoing professional learning of teachers, nevertheless, there are likely to be costs which will have some influence on teachers' classroom performance, their professional engagement and their receptiveness to change. A. Hargreaves (1994) describes the ways in which work intensification occurs in teaching. He argues that intensification leads to a lack of time to retool one's skills and keep up with one's field. It creates chronic and persistent overload (as compared with the temporary overload that is sometimes experienced in meeting deadlines), which reduces areas of personal discretion, inhibits involvement in and control over longer-term planning, and fosters dependency on externally produced materials and expertise. More recently, Smyth *et al.* (2000), in reporting on their study of Appleton College, report that teachers themselves have contributed to their own exploitation. They argue:

> There are many problems for those teachers, which arise from the intensification of their work. They are harassed by the burdens of time with insufficient time to complete all their work tasks in ways that give satisfaction. They have to cut corners in their work by doing essential things first, including a host of administrative and other non-teaching duties, at the expense of creative work like lesson preparation. They

face the potential atrophy of teaching skills through lack of opportunity for engagement with other teachers in professional development and participation in collaborative networks.

(Smyth et al. 2000: 144)

The mandatory application of teacher professional standards on top of teachers' already heavy workload will make the task of teaching even more demanding. There is a danger that, with teachers accepting the challenge of using a standards framework as a source of professional learning, they will become complicit in their own exploitation and the intensification of their work. Acceptance of a standards-based framework for teacher ongoing learning becomes an ideological tool for teachers to do more under the guise of increasing their professionalism and status. Hence professionalism under the guise of standards becomes a tool for employers demanding more of teachers. The implementation of a standards framework puts teachers in a double bind. If they do not have a set of publicly documented standards like other 'professions' then they are seen not to have the same professional status as those professions who do have these codified frameworks. At the same time, by undertaking professional development activities as outlined by Ingvarson (1998c) they contribute to the intensification of their work. For standards to contribute to the ongoing professional learning of teachers, participation in standards-based professional development must be seen as an integral part of teachers' work and time must be allocated for this to occur. While there have been some attempts to extend teachers' working day in schools, or to lengthen the school year (which have, by and large, not been accepted by unions or teachers), a more creative solution needs to be found. One such solution may well be to rethink how schools are organized and how teachers are to work in a more flexible environment. As many have said, the current form of education provision and school organization is an artefact of the Industrial Revolution. What is required now is a form of education provision and delivery which takes into account flexible forms of delivery, different student needs and expectations, and uses resources, both material and intellectual, in more creative and flexible ways. The challenge for those developing standards frameworks is twofold. First, how to accommodate the ambiguities and uncertainties of alternative forms of education provision and policies while at the same time providing teachers and the community with clear guidelines as to what constitutes best practice. Second, how issues of teacher professionalism are debated and developed in order to enhance the quality and status of teaching in order to facilitate and improve student learning. How these are achieved takes the development of teacher professional standards into new and perhaps highly politically charged territory. Dealing with these challenges will require resolve, courage, and political and professional care.

Conclusion

In this chapter I have examined the rhetoric and practices of professional standards for teaching. While not dismissing the value of the development and implementation of professional standards for teaching, especially as a strategy for the continuing professional development of teachers, I do promote the view that there is a need for scepticism and caution, especially with respect to claims made about the benefits of such regimes for the teaching profession and individual teachers. In short, this means questioning what these standards are attempting to do, how this will be done and the overall consequences on teachers' classroom practice.

In a perfect world, any set of professional standards for teaching needs to be owned and overseen by the profession itself. It is politically important that these standards are not primarily self-interested, but rather are concerned with a broader professional project. These standards should not be seen as a government-imposed regulatory framework which promotes one particular view of teaching and what it means to be a teacher. Furthermore, the establishment of professional control, rather than a reactive stance of self-interest, will take time to develop. The development and implementation of professional standards which have currency among both teachers and the broader society is no easy task. Indeed, while there are attempts to align the teaching profession with other professions such as engineers and architects in terms of certification and registration, the uniqueness of the teaching profession must be acknowledged, as must the various contexts in which teaching occurs. While a 'one size fits all' version of standards may be attractive to governments, it may not be in the best interests of teachers teaching in remote areas, in difficult schools, or in multi-age settings where teachers' competency will be judged on the basis of some idealized notion of what competent, or excellent, teaching might be. There needs to be some flexibility regarding the form of the standards to recognize the fact that context plays an important role in influencing how teachers teach, what they teach and the learning outcomes of their students.

The development of standards for teaching is a collective enterprise of all of those who are interested in improving the quality of teaching and student learning outcomes. We have to resist any attempts by those who define teaching too narrowly and work against those who advocate a 'teach to the test' syndrome of a narrow set of teaching attributes. We need to acknowledge that conceptions of good teaching are changing, and that the knowledge and research base of teaching and learning are expanding. This is all occurring at a time when there are significant changes in cultural and social conditions, which impinge on how competent teaching is defined and judged.

Professional standards for teachers which make the distinction between self-interest and self-control have the potential to provide the necessary provocation for teachers to think about their work, classroom activities and professional identity in quite fundamentally different and generative ways. They also provide the potential for teachers to develop a framework to think and talk about their work. Clearly, both developmental and regulatory approaches have their strengths and weaknesses. However, my preference would be more towards the developmental approach than the regulatory one. The expectations and demands of external accountability need to be balanced with the developmental requirements of teachers to improve their practice and improve student learning outcomes. What is required is a variety of opportunities for teachers to achieve this collectively and individually.

Discussing and debating the form, content and effects of professional teaching standards may well provide opportunities for this to happen. The development of professional standards needs to be done by teachers themselves. If this is done, then the standards will have some authenticity in terms of classroom practice and the needs of teachers working in a variety of different contexts. If standards are seen as a set of technical attributes or behaviours that have to be demonstrated out of context then they have little value either for the improvement of classroom practice or for the development of new kinds of teacher professionalism. Furthermore, improvement of classroom practice is more likely to occur where the standards are developed by the teachers themselves and the profession is internally regulated rather than externally controlled. Professional standards must have currency and ownership by those who are to use them – the teachers.

four

Preparing activist teacher professionals

In this chapter I am concerned with identifying some of the issues confronting teacher education faculties in Australia and elsewhere and how those faculties might respond to the challenges of uncertainty and rapid change which confront universities everywhere. My argument is twofold. First, I argue that the development of an activist teaching profession is in the best interests of students, teachers and the broader community. The development of such teachers requires a radical reconceptualization of teacher education programmes, especially as these relate to the content, values and forms of delivery. Second, in order to achieve such outcomes I argue that teacher education faculties must reconceptualize and restructure themselves in a manner that enables them to contribute in collaborative ways to the intellectual and professional leadership of the teaching profession. Implicit in my argument is the view that an activist teacher professional can act as a change agent to improve the quality of education provision, student learning outcomes and the status of teaching as a profession.

In order to undertake this task teacher education faculties need to open themselves up for internal and external scrutiny. In practice this means that they need to constantly ask themselves tough questions about their role in creating the social and intellectual capital required for a dynamic and intelligent teaching profession. I use my experience of the Innovative Links between Schools and Universities Project for Teacher Professional Development and the Master of Teaching programme at the University of Sydney as two examples of how faculties of education can rethink not only their organization but also the professional and social relationships between themselves, schools and systems. The partnership model developed in these examples provided opportunities for teachers, academics, systems and union people to work together for the improvement of teacher learning and professional development.

The changing context of teacher education

The twentieth century experienced more social transformation than any other period in history. To this point, social and cultural transformation has been achieved with relative ease. According to Drucker (1994: 54), 'the age of social transformation will not come to an end with the year 2000 – it will not even have peaked by then'. Most western economies have not been left untouched by these changes. Institutions, workplaces and people's lives are being fundamentally altered by a series of public sector reform strategies aimed at enhancing economic productivity and competitiveness. Not surprisingly, schools and universities are having to respond to these changes in a variety of ways through the demands for them to be more efficient, effective and economic in how they operate at the global and local levels.

In the UK, for example, three major concerns – teacher professionalism, maintaining supply, and creating greater accountability within a national framework for training – have influenced the policy initiatives that have been produced in recent years (Furlong *et al.* 2000). Similarly, externally imposed demands over 'standards' and 'accountability' are at the core of government initiatives in Australia and the USA and have shaped institutional initiatives regarding the assurance of quality programmes and the maintenance and measurement of standards in universities and other educational institutions. Referring to the UK experience in schools, Furlong *et al.* (2000: 6) observe that: 'During the past decade, initiatives such as the introduction of the National Curriculum, league tables, and teacher appraisal (to mention only a few) have served to challenge traditional conceptions of autonomy within the teaching profession'. Directing his comments to schools, but equally applicable to universities, Dalin (1996) suggests that these demands paralyse schools and do not bring them forward. He argues that, 'what we need is a new public debate about the challenges that our students will be facing in their early adult lives and how present societies – and in particular schools – can help to prepare them for the future' (1996: 14). There is evidence to suggest that under the increased regimes of accountability and the development of audit cultures, resources in universities and teacher education faculties have been put under increased pressure by this external scrutiny. Recent demands to respond to quality audits, research audits and the numerous recent enquiries into the role, purpose and outcomes of teacher education faculties have certainly taken energy and time away from the core activities of academic life. For some, the preparation of submissions, documenting processes or putting activities in place that demonstrate the institution's commitment to quality have become the core of their academic work.

In spite of these external demands, the continuing challenge for teacher education faculties is how to prepare teachers for change and to provide them with the requisite knowledge, skills and competencies so that they can contribute to a socially just society. Like schools, teacher education faculties need a new mission in order to be able to respond to rapid change in ways that are productive and generative of new ideas and practices. Smith (2000: 8) makes the telling observation that teacher education has a remarkable capacity to remain fundamentally untouched by waves of social, political and institutional change.

Challenges for teacher education at the institutional and professional levels

If Drucker's perspective that social transformation is ongoing and its potential is yet to be realized is correct, then the implications for teacher education are profound. Teaching in the future will require that we find new and different ways of working within institutions and with the profession in terms of the design and delivery of programmes. Confronted with an 'increasingly post-industrial, post modern world, characterized by accelerating change, intense compression of time and space, cultural diversity, technological complexity, national insecurity and scientific uncertainty' (A. Hargreaves 1994: 4), teachers will be working in conditions where the ability to respond to and manage change will be essential. Dalin (1996: 10) suggests that, 'It is a total misunderstanding that the main orientation of schooling should be to focus solely on the challenges of yesterday and today'. He goes on to argue that 'a school that does not prepare students for the global paradigm shift is an obsolete institution' (1996: 11). A similar logic can be applied to higher education to the extent that a university and a teacher education faculty that does not prepare teachers for this shift will also become obsolete. Add to this the further complexity provided by substantial developments in the use of information communications technology (ICT). As Smith (2000: 8) argues, 'There is abundant evidence now that whatever else information technology might generate, it provides new kinds of life space for young people and access to different kinds of knowledge and experience'. It certainly behoves teacher education programmes to be mindful of the experience and understanding of students use of ICT.

The challenge, then, for education faculties is to prepare teachers for the future who are able to negotiate the complexities of what is referred to as a knowledge society (Drucker 1994). Education will become the centre of a knowledge society, and the school its key institution. In a knowledge society, more and more knowledge, especially advanced knowledge, will be acquired well past the age of formal schooling and, increasingly, through education processes that do not centre on the traditional school. This has important consequences for the form and structure of teacher education programmes. Indeed, as new communication technologies are increasingly used to deliver education programmes, new kinds of knowledge and experience will have to be integrated into teacher education programmes. Furthermore, the universities' monopoly over knowledge and its transmission will be challenged. For Grimmett (1995), this requires that universities reconceptualize their mission as preparing revitalized teachers for revitalized schools. To achieve this, teacher educators will have to align themselves with systemic reform of schools and systematically seek out partnerships with other interested groups, both from within the university and from outside it (Grimmett 1995). Failure to do so will exacerbate the discontent which is felt by some schools and systems which perceive that their interests are not served in the present arrangements for teacher education (Smith 2000).

School systems are regularly being restructured and policies for education reform are being promulgated with monotonous regularity. Most education systems in Australia and elsewhere have been restructured since the late 1990s or are undergoing restructuring. Within the context of continual change, 'more and more will be expected of future teachers, whether it be a question of ethical training, training for tolerance or the ability to manage uncertainty, creativity, solidarity or participation' (Tedesco 1996: 1). The question then is, are teacher education institutions up to the challenge of preparing teachers who can respond to change in creative and responsible ways? My unequivocal response is yes, but with two qualifications: (1) teacher education should not be owned by the university; it should be recognized that it is the joint property of the university and the profession, and (2) restructuring alone is not enough, teacher education faculties have to reconceptualize their place in the professional world and how they operate within that world. Central to both of these points is the need for teacher education faculties to establish different kinds of professional and practical relationships with their colleagues in schools, systems and unions. In many respects there is a need develop an Accord between these groups so that industrial and professional issues and issues of practice can be debated and clarified. One role the university might take on is to provide intellectual and professional leadership. I take this point up later.

Teacher education institutions are faced with a conundrum. While they prepare students to teach in continually changing schools and systems, as organizations they have not, until recently, been subjected to such politically motivated ongoing reform. As Grimmett (1995: 205) observes, 'the reform of schools occurs independently of teacher education. No incentive exists to bring the two together and the gap appears to be widening'. For many working in schools, the gap between theory and practice as represented by academics and school-based practitioners is widening. Academic knowledge, for some, does not have the same currency as practitioner knowledge. Accordingly, credibility is an issue for university staff in the eyes of many school-based practitioners. This situation of wariness presents different kinds of challenges for school-based practitioners and academics. For school-based practitioners it means that they have to confront the limits of their own context, subject and pedagogical knowledge and practice. Their credibility rests with their school-based peers. Academics face different expectations and demands. They have to meet and respond to the expectations of their university peers, both from inside their own faculties and from other faculties within the university. At the same time they have to maintain links with schools and the teaching profession. The tension between academic knowledge and practitioner knowledge is played out regularly when university students visit schools for the practicum. All too often, students attending practice are faced with the prejudice against theory, as represented by university learning, and are told by their supervisors, 'don't listen to what they tell you at university – the real knowledge and learning happens here'. This response is counterproductive. It serves to fracture and fragment the view that the teaching profession is a learning profession and it obscures the view that teacher educators should be practising and modelling excellence in terms of teaching and student learning outcomes. However, it does speak of the need to question a persuasive assumption within the ranks of teacher educators and of the misplaced hegemony of university-based teacher education in the provision and delivery of programmes to train teachers. As Smith (2000: 12) puts it, 'teacher educators claim privilege for the university leadership role in teacher education, whereas it can just as easily be construed as self-interest'.

Importantly, within a context of rethinking teacher educators' place in the world, the denigrating of areas of expertise within the profession works against the development of collegial relationships between teachers and their academic colleagues. Such relationships in their best forms serve to improve the knowledge base of teaching, enhance student learning outcomes and contribute to the renewal and revisioning of the teaching profession.

One way forward is to develop faculties of education based on a different set of assumptions and social relations, where the fundamental values are enquiry, development, engagement and improvement. Such faculties are informed by an ethos that promotes the development of new kinds of relationships between various groups whose core business is education in its broadest sense. Opportunities are created that actively promote the production and circulation of new kinds of knowledge and different kinds of practice. Finally, the new ethos is concerned with the establishment of a risk-taking culture whereby experimenting with the use of a variety of strategies and opportunities for teachers and academics to work together in mutually beneficial ways is rewarded and becomes part of 'the way we do things around here'. Such a risk-taking culture complements a culture of enquiry that comes under close scrutiny by students, teachers and academics alike. Each of these assumptions and values, individually and collectively, is concerned with the improvement of practice and the development of new kinds of teacher professionalism. In such a faculty, which includes academics, practitioners, union officials and so on, all members recognize that they possess different kinds of expertise, knowledge and skills, and that when this is shared it contributes to student learning and the enhancement of the teaching profession with both short-term and long-term implications.

Challenges for teacher education at the political and social levels

Within the current political and economic climate the challenges for university-based teacher education involve issues of accountability and competency. They may be summarized as follows:

1 Pressure of external accountability from a variety of education stakeholders.
2 Increased political pressure to direct the processes, structures and qualifications of teacher preparation.
3 Demands for school-based teacher education programmes.
4 The provision of more economical and efficient teacher education programmes, and the preparation of competent practitioners.

Within the Australian context, in 1998 the reports of three national initiatives were published: the Senate Inquiry into the Status of Teaching; the West Inquiry into Higher Education; and the National Standards and Guidelines for Initial Teacher Education. These reports have the potential to deeply influence teacher education. Indeed, much effort went into responses to these initiatives by teacher education faculties and the teaching profession. While any one of these initiatives could be the impetus for externally imposed restructuring, paradoxically none of these federally developed initiatives has been supported by government through changes in policy or the allocation of funds. It could be said that, despite the anxiety of the profession about some of the recommendations contained in the reports, nothing substantial has yet occurred to require a dramatic change in teacher education practices.

The challenge for teacher education faculties, then, is to see these initiatives as opportunities rather than threats and to reconceptualize their mission and their place in the world. These external initiatives demand that teacher education faculties become proactive by rethinking their programmes and their relationships with the teaching profession, rather than engaging in an internally oriented and reactive activity restructuring in response to these initiatives. Tom (1997: 223–4) makes the strong argument that:

> Teacher educators need to establish a base for socially negotiating collective answers to diverse faces of teacher education reform.... Teacher educators need to change, but change is also needed in our work settings, in the ways that schools and universities are linked.

This is an important point because it demands that significant changes be made within universities regarding how the work of teacher educators is understood and rewarded. The latter has special force in that for many teacher educators the professional work that they do with schools does not fit well with the types of research profile usually demanded by promotion committees.

According to Grimmett (1995), restructuring without reconceptualization does not lead to genuine change in teacher education. The current education climate demands change rather than adjustment. What has occurred all too frequently in teacher education faculties is that programmes have been adjusted to respond to the immediate demands of internal and external pressures. Because the need to be seen to be responsive to these pressures requires an immediate strategy, there is a tendency to make adjustments around the edges, change the names of a few units of study, adjust the amount of time spent in schools, and even to introduce a couple of new units so that the institution is seen to respond to government policy pressures.

In the current political and social climate it is contingent upon teacher education faculties to move away from reactive responses and to think in strategic and divergent ways in order to be able to respond to these pressures. Restructuring needs to be done within the wider context of debate and resolution about what is the place of teacher education faculties within universities and what is their core business? These issues speak of the need for restructuring and reconceptualizing to be simultaneous and complementary activities. This has both immediate and long-term implications. Grimmett (1995: 210) puts it well when he argues:

> restructuring arising from a fundamental reconceptualization of how to prepare teachers not only brings about educationally defensible changes in teacher education practices but it also alters the outcomes, producing a teacher capable of entering the workforce with a much clearer initial grasp of the issues and complexity involved in teaching in today's rapidly changing social context.

In this chapter I am concerned with looking critically at the dual tasks of reconceptualizing and restructuring at the level of the profession in order to develop an activist teacher professional. I argue that new forms of professional affiliations and partnerships must be initiated in the conceptualization, design, delivery and future development of education programmes. People who represent various interest groups, stakeholders and consumers of education programmes and research must be involved in this project. At the pedagogical level, how knowledge is organized and delivered is at issue. There is a synergy between the two so that the experiences and practices of one constantly inform and reform the other.

Taking on Grimmett's challenge of the need to reconceptualize teacher education programmes, I identify two strategies that contribute to such a broad professional project. The first is the development of new kinds of relationships across the profession, one of which is school–university partnerships. Here I concur strongly with Tom's (1997: 224) position:

> Faculties of teacher education must work with others in our settings to redesign teacher education. Reform is at root a localistic enterprise even though many conceptual and structural commonalities may be found across sites. Our most fundamental commonality is the moral imperative to act. Without vigorous action, we teacher educators will be culpable and just deserve to be blamed for the shortcomings of teacher education.

This call to action is the trigger for my rethinking teacher education as a general enterprise. Furthermore it suggests the need for 'interruptions' to our taken-for-granted assumptions and the conventional wisdom that has shaped much of our thinking and responses to the changing needs and expectations of the community and the teaching profession itself.

The second area of concern is the development of what Smith (2000) refers to as a platform approach to teacher education. A platform approach seeks novelty and builds service into a political agenda aimed at social justice for student teachers and schoolchildren. It opens possibilities for new knowledge and pedagogies that are more flexible, task-oriented and responsive to learner needs than tends to be the case in the conventional model (Smith 2000: 22). In several respects the platform approach puts many of the uncontested assumptions about the resourcing and development of teacher education programmes up for scrutiny. It is worth quoting Smith (2000: 23) at some length:

> In the platform approach, the calculation and distribution of costs shifts to design of platform upgrading because the platform in a sense *is* the program. The platform mindset is concerned with providing the best possible program for students rather than with what 'fits' university

accounting systems. In turn, the platform approach encourages more adventurous mindsets that redefine 'problems' as opportunities, that create management and organizational models structured by what has to be done rather than by internally and externally imposed bureaucratic rules and formula finding.

University–school partnerships are fundamental to reconceptualizing teacher education programmes. In many cases these partnerships provide the impetus and sustenance for reform and change processes within schools and teacher education faculties. The challenges facing teacher education have not occurred within a political or policy vacuum, rather they are part of a broad suite of education reforms. Before indicating what a reconceptualized teacher education might look like it is important to briefly examine the general intent of teacher education reform.

Teacher education reform

Pressure to change the form, content and outcomes of teacher education programmes have been long-standing. Various state-mandated enquiries into initial and continuing teacher education have occurred regularly over the past twenty years in Australia, the UK and USA. On many occasions they have been instigated as a result of continuing criticism of the quality and relevance of teacher education programmes which have come from teachers themselves, students, employing authorities and governments. Reform of teacher education, then, is not straightforward. As Tom (1997: 2) argues, 'The problem of reform has political and institutional roots, not just intellectual and conceptual ones.' The problem is complex, and solutions have the added difficulty of having to meet the needs and expectations of a variety of interest groups and stakeholders.

Despite this complexity there are some features common to all aspects of reform of teacher education. Fullan *et al.* (1998: 58) identify the following:

- A stronger knowledge base for teaching and teacher education;
- Attracting able, diverse, and committed students to the career of teaching;
- Redesigning teacher preparation programs so that the linkages to arts and sciences, and the field of practice, are strengthened;
- Reform in the working conditions of schools;
- The development and monitoring of standards for programs as well as for teacher candidates and teachers on the job; and
- A rigorous and dynamic research enterprise focusing on teaching, teacher education, and on the assessment and monitoring of strategies.

On the surface these appear to be clear enough. Why, then, has the enterprise of reforming teacher education been so difficult to progress? Perhaps the answer lies in the fact that different groups have conflicting agendas and outcomes when it comes to teacher education reform. The state, especially through education bureaucracies, is concerned with external accountability. Unions focus on industrial agendas, especially those that relate to remuneration and working conditions. For teachers and parents, improvements in student learning and in the conditions in which teachers and students work are central interests.

Fullan *et al.* (1998) suggest that many initiatives to reform teacher education have stalled. Referring specifically to the reform work of the North American Holmes Group, they observe that even though there are some pockets of success, the Holmes Group began to lose focus and momentum, particularly in the mid-1990s:

> By the time *Tomorrow's Schools of Education* finally appeared, many readers were disappointed to find that what they saw as bromides and 'polemical prose' that provided little concrete help in reforming schools of teacher education and seemed to underplay critical components of the reform agenda.
>
> (Fullan et al. 1998: 39)

This is disappointing. As Smith and Weaver (1998: 40) argue, the potential offered by new reform initiatives has not in the main been taken up, and the types of response to these initiatives are predictable:

> adapting to new pressures under the guise of numerous teacher education course restructures and policy revisions without internal reconceptualization and the welding of external political alliances, has diverted the attention of teacher education from accountability and responsiveness. Widespread contemporary attempts to bring teachers, schools, systems and the universities closer operationally and to establish industry-wide guidelines are predictable responses by providers to perceived threats, albeit well-intentioned. The proposed initiatives, however, remain in the existing model of teacher education and within standard policy practices rather than providing a holistic logic for the future of teacher education.

Various strategies have been used in the drive to reform teacher education in Australia and elsewhere. Tom (1997) identifies four change strategies which he has observed in the USA, but which are equally appropriate for the reform initiatives occurring elsewhere. These are:

- the establishment of a task force (a broadly representative group plans a new program);

- top down (the provost told us to join the Holmes Group or state standards require two courses of reading methods);
- pilot program (a new program is attempted by a subset of the faculty and students);
- family style (a faculty continually meets and discusses how to proceed).

(Tom 1997: 163–4)

These strategies may be familiar to education reformers. Some may have been used as an independent strategy, whereas others may have been used in combination to reinforce each other. For example, it is possible to envisage that a taskforce is established to investigate possible models for a new programme, but the motivation to do so has come from a change in state or national education policy or accreditation requirements. When there are strong coercive forces behind an initiative it is not surprising that pragmatism is the response. Readjusting rather than reconceptualizing is the likely outcome.

Reconceptualizing teacher education programmes

Improving the quality of education depends on improving the recruitment, selection, training, and social status and work conditions of teachers. Teachers need appropriate knowledge and skills, personal characteristics, professional prospects and motivation if they are to meet the expectations placed on them (Delor 1996: 142). One of the primary outcomes of any teacher education programme should be educating and skilling intellectually reflective and strategic practitioners. These are teachers who can work both collaboratively and independently, are able to solve complex practical and theoretical problems, are able to reflect on their practice in order to develop quality learning opportunities for their students, and finally are professionals who are able to cope with rapid social and technological change. In order to develop and sustain the teaching profession, teacher education programmes need to establish and expand the knowledge and skills base to make the difference in the lives of the students they teach as well as develop and practise the knowledge and skills required to change organizations.

Reconceptualizing professional relationships

In order to meet contemporary challenges it is necessary to establish different kinds of relationships and partnerships with various educational stakeholders and to investigate alternative forms of educational provision and delivery. The importance of partnerships is captured well by a teacher participating in the Innovative Links project:

> Partnerships have great value as they break down the isolation teachers and schools have within the total community of educators. Teachers have little or no contact with universities other than practicums.

This quote provides both academics and teachers with a clear picture of the opportunities and benefits of developing partnerships. It highlights the need for both parties to look outside their own domain and to build a community of interest whereby education issues and practices are debated and strategies implemented. It is suggestive of new forms of professional and personal association. For this to work it has to based on reciprocity, where both parties meet on equal grounds, with the desire to improve student learning outcomes and teacher practice at its core. At the same time it must be acknowledged that the development of a partnership needs to be based on the identification of a mutual need.

The idea of partnerships between various groups interested in improving the quality of education is not new. There is a burgeoning literature that extols the virtues of school–university partnerships and the contribution they make to teacher professional development at the school and system levels, to reforming schools' and universities' practices and procedures, and finally bringing relevance to educational research. My interest here, though, is in terms of the operation of the partnerships in general and the micro political dynamics of their enactment.

These new relationships, among others, would include using the expertise of practitioner teachers in the design of individual subjects and courses, advisory groups of teachers, union members and systems people. In some faculties this is already happening, but it needs to become widespread. By establishing these partnerships, new professional and practical relationships are established. Both parties see their roles as contributing to the improvement of practice and the development of a knowledge base about teaching. Both parties provide different perspectives and strategies for improving practice and student learning outcomes.

The experience of the Innovative Links project demonstrated that successful partnerships have the following characteristics: collaborative, mutually respectful, supportive and providing mutual resource support (Yeatman and Sachs 1995). They demand the development of trust, respect and new forms of work practice.

For partnerships to be successful, a fundamental tension about roles and purposes for the partnership needs to be resolved. On the one hand, the development of partnerships between university-based staff and school-based staff with a view to fostering the professional development of teachers, could be characterized as one where the academics' role is one of facilitating such development. Here, expertise is possessed by the academics, with the teachers as recipients of that expertise. On the other hand,

and a much more fruitful model, is the development of a partnership between university-based staff and school-based staff where the continuing professional development of both teachers and academics is the purpose of the partnership.

The model of association encapsulated in the first aim is one of expert–client, where the power relationships between the two parties are unequal, and academic/theoretical knowledge is privileged over practitioner knowledge. The model inherent in the second aim is more collaborative and equal. Both parties are positioned to interact as learners to the extent that the knowledge of academics and practitioners is perceived by both as complementary (Yeatman and Sachs 1995).

With the first model, partnership is a word used to describe a one-way flow of exchange and support. The relationship is designed to assist the professional growth and learning of teachers. In this conception of partnership, the teacher educator academic's professionalism is left unproblematized, and it is associated with the traditional conception of a professional service mission. It is the role of the teacher educator to give support to teachers in schools. While this is a worthy ambition, as long as it is left within an unreconstructed ethos of professional service, it must risk a drift into the kind of paternalism that is associated with the traditional service role (Yeatman and Sachs 1995), that is the power relations between the academics and teachers are left unquestioned and inevitably lead to an expert–client model of association. Furthermore, it fails to recognize expertise as it relates to the practice of those working in schools.

The first model leaves two important questions unasked. First, what do academics/universities gain by providing this service of facilitation, when, in many cases this is on top of their normal load. Second, why is this relationship not conceived as a horizontal or lateral relationship of reciprocal exchange and learning?

The second model represents a two-way model of reciprocity, that is in essence experimental and with some risk since for many it embodies a new relationship between the two and a different mode of operating within and outside of schools. This model assumes that each party has something to contribute to the professional learning of the other. In particular, it assumes that university-based teacher education needs to be in a reciprocal learning relationship with school-based teacher education and development.

The purpose of a reciprocal form of association between academics and teachers is threefold. First, both parties are concerned with building joint endeavours and promoting collaborative development. Through building joint endeavours, teachers and academic associates are involved in extending how both parties work in schools and universities alike. As Thiessen (1992) suggests, this entails more than redistributing labour or capitalizing on the labour of others; it means that both parties search for possibilities and alternatives, and in all this they learn from their interactions. At the core of this interaction is the possibility for exchanging expertise. Second, by promoting collaborative development, both teachers and academics are given the opportunity to elaborate practical theories. This allows them to examine the relationship between their espoused theories and their theories in use to define and direct their separate and shared improvement. In so doing, teachers and academics generate and sustain the energy for change within their evolving relationship. Finally, such practices enhance professional dialogue, the purpose of which is to generate analytical insights into, and improvements of, classroom practices (Yeatman and Sachs 1995).

The benefits of reconceptualizing the professional relationships between school- and university-based staff are captured in the following quote gained during the evaluation of the Innovative Links project. Here an academic is reflecting on the individual and collective benefits of academics working more closely with the profession:

> I (and my university colleagues) am attempting to break down the perception of University teacher educators as out of touch, elitist, privileged and irrelevant boffins. We acknowledge the complexity of schools' and teachers' work, we promote teachers researching their own problems, and we seek partnerships with them in the process. We try to demonstrate the same skills and abilities required by many school-based teachers – the ability to work collaboratively, to negotiate process as well as outcome, to be socially critical and overtly moral.

Both formally and informally, partnerships between university-based staff and school-based staff afford the opportunity to develop a 'community of practice' (Lave and Wenger 1991). Fundamental to this is the assumption that social practice – what practitioners do and how they talk about what they do – is the primary generative phenomenon, with learning one of its characteristics. From this perspective, 'learning not in the acquisition of structure, but in the increased access of learners to participating roles in expert performance' (Lave and Wenger 1991: 17). Expert performance is certainly a central outcome of any teacher education or professional development programme. Central to this is the ability to talk about it, to tell stories about it, not as a second-order representation of what to do but as an integral part of what it is to be an expert performer. Learning is thus a way of *being* in a particular social world, not merely knowing about it or describing it (Lave and Wenger 1991).

Within a community of practice, emphasis is placed upon participation in a community of practitioners, rather than merely the acquisition of a set of skills or practices deemed to satisfy bureaucratic requirements. Partnership between academics and school-based practitioners is a two-way process and requires flexibility on the part of both groups. It involves listening to the stories about practice, feeding the stories back in the form of observations, questions, and so on so that participants are involved in an ongoing conversation about practice. In Somekh's (1994) words, it points to the need to 'inhabit each other's castles'. Both parties move from peripheral involvement in the development and improvement process of teaching to one of full participation. A conversation is initiated about learning, and how people can learn from each other, especially when they work collaboratively in school-based projects. This conversation becomes an integral part of the activities of the community of practice. It is ongoing, and while there will be interruptions when the exigencies and pressures of school and classroom life get in way, these learnings can be returned to, reflected upon and used to provoke new conversations, perceptions and positions. However, this conversation does require a commitment in terms of time and energy by all members of the school or education community to sustain it.

Let me now provide an example of a community of practice that has emerged through the Innovative Links between Schools and Universities Project for Teacher Professional Development. In many of these projects there was view shared by teachers and academics that collaboration of various kinds provided a mechanism for the development of new forms of association between school-based personnel and university staff.

At the core of reconceptualized teacher education is the need to change the relational and pedagogical aspects of programme design and delivery. It necessitates a shared desire of academics and school-based personnel to develop socially critical practitioners who can make a contribution to the practice and theory of teaching. Furthermore, it is underscored by acknowledging that new roles and responsibilities will have to be negotiated and made explicit between these two groups. To achieve this, notions of expertise will have to be debated. New forms of affiliation between academics and school-based practitioners will have to be instigated for the mutual enhancement of education theory and practice. Learning, as a common endeavour, and the desire to improve student learning outcomes through improved practice will be the common ground for this to occur. However, this will have to be done in a climate where risk-taking is acknowledged and mistakes are considered to be part of the learning process. It will require that a conversation is initiated between academics and school-based practitioners, and processes which will sustain a commitment to continue are put in place. If these initiatives are undertaken by both academics and school-based practitioners then teacher education can be reconceptualized and university faculties restructured in mutually complementary ways. The outcome of this activity will be the development of a more active, informed and socially responsible teaching profession.

Teacher educators working towards an activist teaching profession

A reconceptualized teacher education programme will have at its centre a strong statement about the types of activity that teacher educators can carry out in professional and academic arenas. It means recasting the role and influence of teacher educators more broadly. Accordingly, the question that needs to be asked is, how can those responsible for the initial and continuing education of teachers advise and support the profession? In answering this question I identify six areas where teacher educators and education faculties can be proactive in the development of an activist teaching profession. Importantly, the suggestions that I make have direct implications for the work of teacher educators, especially the role that individuals and institutions have in renewing teacher professionalism and developing activist teacher professionals. Activist teacher educators can be involved in the following:

1 advising
2 issue and problem identification
3 spreading ideas
4 providing alternative perspectives
5 evaluating programmes
6 advocacy.

Advising

Teacher educators have a variety of areas of expertise. These include an understanding of various approaches to education research, policy and practice. Reconceputalized teacher education programmes also locate them both structurally and professionally in a strong position to provide advice to governments, schools and systems. Given that, in Australia, there is evidence indicating that most education research is undertaken in universities or by independent researchers, the role of teacher educators in advising various constituencies is significant.

Issue and problem identification

Research with teachers or on aspects of education policy and practice can identify the existence of emerging issues or recurrent problems. The effect is twofold. One is the creation of debate about the issues or problems across a range of stakeholder or interest groups; and the other is the resolution of the problem through a policy response or some other method of formal intervention. By attempting to be a disinterested broker, a variety of solutions may emerge, which in turn help to foster rigorous debate and intellectual activity.

Spreading ideas

The notion of an activist teaching professional is, for some, an idea whose time has come. But ideas need to be explained and disseminated, and most importantly they need champions or advocates. Teacher educators are in a strong position to do this, especially when they are working in collaboration with other stakeholders. The role of teacher education in the initial socialization of neophyte teachers and the issuing of credentials to teachers, positions them strongly to spread new ideas and be part of the process that enables such ideas to emerge through the work of expanded communities of practice.

Providing alternative perspectives

If there is a problem at either the system or the school level that relates to policy or practice, what can the possible options be and how can they be fine-tuned? Education systems and bureaucracies have problems suggesting new ideas, especially if they are seen to be at variance with current government policy directions. Teacher educators, acting either individually or collectively with other stakeholders, including parent bodies, can present a variety of possibilities without being dismissed for their audacity. If teacher educators can build strong links with various interest groups then governments may look to them for advice and assistance.

Evaluating programmes

Evaluations can often be difficult and fraught with tension on the part of those commissioning the evaluations and those undertaking them. An evaluation may reveal that a programme is unsuccessful according to all criteria, but still the logic of the programme must be upheld. Academics can participate in evaluating programmes not only to give the programme legitimacy but also to provide feedback regarding how it might be improved. Because academic discourse *is* different from that of government, evaluation can provide an independent account of what is happening at various levels of practice. Its distance from policy and government may also enable viewpoints or alternative models to be presented and debated which in the long term may provide quite different opportunities or outcomes.

Advocacy

Advocacy occurs across a variety of constituencies: teachers, students and the profession. Again, teacher educators can act as advocates because they have access to information and networks to disseminate that information. They can also be seen as independent commentators. The process of engaging in advocacy requires a well-thought-out strategy for engagement and communication. As Apple (2000) notes, we can learn a great deal about mobilizing public opinion from the strategies that the political right has utilized to frame public opinion, from various issues ranging from 'right to life' to the 'decline in education standards'.

Teacher education for an activist teaching profession

A teacher education programme to prepare an activist teaching profession would have many of the characteristics that Liston and Zeichner (1991) identified under the rubric of their social reconstructionist approach. It is disappointing that many of the ideas presented in the early 1990s are yet to find their way into many teacher education programmes. It is worth revisiting some of the elements of a social reconstructionist approach to teacher education.

A social reconstructionist teacher education programme or one to produce activist teacher professionals requires a strong articulation between the structure, organization and delivery of the programmes, course content, and the pedagogy and social relations that are integral to its delivery. In many instances, ensuring that the whole programme is an aggregate of all of its parts will require substantial changes in the philosophy and structure of the teacher education programme. This provides further evidence of the need to reconceptualize rather than make adjustments around the edges.

However, equally as important is the development of a common set of assumptions which will advise the form and content of the programme. My own work as part of a team to teach in the Master of Teaching programme at the University of Sydney has provided me with a variety of experiences that have provoked my thinking and practices about a new kind of teacher education programme. In what follows I outline some of the assumptions that have emerged from my own reflections and discussion with my University of Sydney colleagues. I have used these as the basis of my thinking about the conceptual and operational scaffolding for a teacher education programme to produce activist teacher professionals.

Education is political

It seems obvious to say that education is political. What counts as curriculum knowledge, how schools and education programmes are resourced, who has influence in the development of policy agendas, are all dimensions of the political nature of education policy and practices. The development of education policy and how these policies are enacted in schools are all sites of struggle, with various interest groups vying for the control of meaning and practice. Schools are, as Mahony and Hextall (2000) argue, political institutions.

> They both reflect and reconstitute (or challenge) social inequalities organized around the axes of 'race', gender, class, sexuality and disability. What Connell (1993) has called the 'political order' of the school is mediated through patterns of teaching and non-teaching staff employment; the messages conveyed in curriculum materials; the organisation of option choices; the basis on which students are grouped; teaching and assessment practices; the assumptions embedded in school discipline; the organisation of the pastoral system; the kinds of language used and the ways interpersonal relations are handled.
>
> (Mahony and Hextall 2000: 123)

Similarly, teacher education is political, both internally and externally. Its place and status in universities is variable. In some universities there are large and relatively well resourced faculties, whereas in others, teacher education is located in small departments which are vying with other departments in the faculty not only for resources but also for visibility. Reid *et al.* (1998) make a compelling argument for the need for teacher education programmes to develop teachers who have highly developed political skills. Such a programme will have to develop political sensibilities that will enable teachers

> to struggle in the various arenas where policy is determined, to wrest back and then maintain some greater degree of autonomy in their curriculum work. This will require the capacity to recognise the way curriculum operates, the critical skills to uncover hegemonic constructions of teaching as an apolitical activity, and the will to work collectively, through union and professional associations, to do something about it. It requires political understandings including knowledge about how and where educational policy is shaped, who to target in political campaigns, and how education unions and political parties work. And it demands a significant array of political skills, including the capacity to negotiate, advocate, lobby, communicate and organise in the wider political arena.
>
> (Reid *et al.* 1998: 252)

The challenge, then, is to provide teachers with the understanding and skills that will enable them to operate effectively in political environments. These environments may be the schools in which they are working, but more likely the communities in which these schools are located. Effective communication, problem-solving and advocacy are some of the skills that will enable teachers to be activists in their own professional lives and to enliven public interest and the debate in the broader education enterprise.

Enquiry into practice

Enquiry stands at the centre of all activities in developing an activist teacher. As Liston and Zeichner (1991) argue, teaching itself can be seen as a form of enquiry. In a programme to develop the activist teacher, professional teachers are viewed as researchers of their own practices, capable of producing worthwhile knowledge about teaching which can contribute to their own and others' professional development. The role of teacher research as a vehicle to revitalize teacher professionalism is taken up in the next chapter; suffice it to say here, though, that developing the skills to help teachers enquire into their own and others' practice is fundamental to an activist-oriented teacher education programme. Enquiry must be seen to be a fundamental aspect of any teacher education programme, and the opportunity to communicate the results of such enquiry to a wide range of audiences – peer, practitioner and academic – must be encouraged.

Learning-centred programmes

Learning rather than teaching and content should be the focus of an activist teacher education programme. By making learning the focus rather than teaching, the social relations of on-campus learning are fundamentally changed. Both students and teacher educators see that the interactions that occur in classrooms become part of a body of intellectual and experiential knowledge that can be interrogated and debated. They provide a foundation for the circulation of new kinds of professional knowledge and insight.

The Master of Teaching programme in my own faculty at the University of Sydney is an example of a programme that is attempting to develop teachers who are change agents. This is a two-year postgraduate programme which uses an interdisciplinary enquiry-based approach utilizing cases from practice. Many of the cases have been written by teachers working in schools and provide the main framework for the course rather than one segment of it (Ewing and Smith 1999). The use of the case-based framework implies that every student teacher's experience on entering the course and during it will be unique. In each phase of the course, student teachers are encouraged to adopt a socially critical and reflective approach to teaching. Questions of equity and the effects of different pedagogies on student learning are examined through the lenses of race, ethnicity, class, gender and sexuality. The use of information technology both as a tool for student learning and as a means for students to communicate with one another is an important feature of the course. Course materials are available on the website, as are other resources. Students are also encouraged to engage in online, virtual discussions. A virtual classroom is under development as a learning resource for students.

Students are encouraged to keep a diary of their learning over the two years of the programme, consisting of both campus-based and school-based reflections and professional development. This forms part of their learning portfolio, one of the forms of assessment used in the programme. Although the diaries are private, entries from them form the basis of some assessment tasks.

The programme concludes with a ten-week internship. As part of this internship, student teachers are expected to engage in an action research project. The findings of these projects are shared with the Master of Teaching cohort at a student forum. Students who have undertaken their internship in an overseas site and are not on campus for the research forum are expected to present their research and engage in discussion with their peers over the Internet. Staff and students are actively encouraged to attend, with the general consensus from students that much can be gained by sharing their research findings.

Collaboration and partnership

As indicated earlier in this chapter, partnerships and collaboration are a central platform in the project of an activist teacher education. Furlong *et al.* (2000: 77–8) identify what they describe as ideal typical models of partnership. The continuum they present ranges from collaborative partnership at one end of the scale to complementary partnership at the other. These two types of partnership represent two very different strategies for linking work in schools with that of teacher educators and other interested parties. According to Furlong *et al.* (2000), in a complementary partnership the school and the university are seen as having separate and complementary responsibilities but there is no attempt to bring these two dimensions into dialogue. Alternatively, a collaborative partnership

> requires the commitment by teacher educators and school-based practitioners to develop a program 'where students are exposed to different forms of educational knowledge, some of which come from the school, some of which come from higher education or elsewhere. Teachers are seen as having an equally legitimate but perhaps different body of professional knowledge from those in higher education. Students are expected and encouraged to build up their own body of professional knowledge.
>
> (Furlong *et al.* 2000: 80)

In order to institutionalize collaborative partnerships and embed them into the culture and practices of schools and teacher education faculties, a strong commitment to develop what Nias *et al.* (1989) refer to as 'cultures of collaboration' is required. These cultures of collaboration are informal as well as formal, intermingle personal and professional life, and are often constructed in the interstices of school life through conversation, shared glances and many kinds of joint work. Not surprisingly, many of the outcomes of partnerships emerge not from the planned or intended strategies, but rather by happenstance and serendipity.

The list below is indicative of some possible outcomes facilitated by partnerships and collaborative relationships between teacher educators and others:

- negotiated expectations
- collaborative planning
- sharing of expertise
- diversity of perspectives and view points
- knowledge generation
- development of trust.

Importantly, though, in order to develop collaborative partnerships we must not underestimate the high level of trust and mutual respect that this entails. Without trust and respect, partnerships are on very shaky ground.

Conclusion

In this chapter I have identified some of the pressures that educational reforms have placed on the provision of teacher education programmes in Australia and elsewhere. I have argued that for far too long teacher education faculties have not put their programmes under close scrutiny or critical examination and, as a consequence, they have not made revisions to the form, content or assumptions informing their programmes that would enable them to be seen to be relevant and contemporary by their colleagues working in schools. With the rapid rate and extent of social change now occurring, we have reached an historical moment where it is imperative to radically revise how teachers are educated. This will demand that we fundamentally rethink the types of programme that will provide new teachers with the requisite intellectual and professional skills. By giving teachers a strong intellectual foundation, reconceptualized teacher education programmes will enable new teachers to deal with the complexities of change and enable them to work in schools that are likely to be different from their current formations.

I have drawn on my own experiences as a teacher educator to present some ideas that will move us beyond what Smith (2000) refers to as the conventional model. Importantly, I see that teacher education and teacher educators have a central role in the development of new kinds of teacher professionalism. Through a socially critical form of teacher education that is predicated on learning, partnerships, collaboration and risk-taking, the rise of an activist teacher professional is possible. This will not occur over night, but if there are exemplars of an activist form of teacher professionalism in place and teacher education faculties provide the intellectual leadership, then an activist teacher professionalism led by teacher educators, with the support of a variety of stakeholders, becomes a reality. It is my hope that this will be led by the profession, with multiple constituencies, and become recognized as the norm rather than as a social experiment. For a strong teaching force we need a strong teacher education. To achieve this we need a teacher education that is contemporary, rigorous and intellectually demanding. In practice this may mean that some will be left by the wayside and that new staff members enter into teacher education faculties. It is a future to be excited about, but one in which teacher educators, individually and collectively, must take intellectual and moral leadership. In other words, the onus lies on teacher educators to create an alternative agenda regarding debates and policies for teacher education and to identify opportunities for a future for the teaching profession that is activist in its orientation.

five

Teacher research for professional renewal

For the past few years there has been an increasing pressure on teachers to undertake 'research' in their own classrooms or schools either with school-based peers or with academic colleagues. This research has variously come under the banner of 'teacher research', 'practitioner research', 'collaborative enquiry' or 'action research'. In general, the purpose of these activities is fourfold: (1) as a strategy for a broader change initiative within a school or classroom; (2) the improvement of classroom practice; (3) as a contribution to an understanding of the nature of teachers' knowledge base; and (4) as a basis for teacher professional development. The research is often done collaboratively with academic colleagues in order to systematically investigate aspects of classroom practice. While I acknowledge that there are differences between these terms, I will generally use 'teacher research' for the sake of simplicity and clarity when referring to these various forms of school-based enquiry. My aim in this chapter is twofold. First, to describe the nature and scope of initiatives that come under the rubric of teacher research, and second, to identify some of the issues I have experienced as they relate to teacher research as a professional development activity for teachers and academics which contributes to revitalizing teacher professionalism along activist lines.

What is teacher research?

Since the late 1990s, the experience of initiatives undertaken through the auspices of the National Schools Network (NSN) and the Innovative Links between Schools and Universities Project has provided a template for what

is possible when school-based practitioners and academics work collaboratively in the enterprise of classroom- or school-based research. However,
this kind of research practice is not without its critics or its problems. For
example, the position taken by Huberman (1996) and Cochran-Smith and
Lytle (1998) provide two quite opposite views of the field. Huberman (1996)
engages in a trenchant critique of the field and brings into question whether
teacher research is research at all, by challenging the claim that it may be
thought of as a new genre or that teacher research may have the potential
to generate a 'qualitatively distinctive body of understandings, skills and
dispositions' (1996: 124). Huberman's position is that if teacher research is
research at all, then it is located within what he describes as the 'fairly
classic genre' of interpretive research (cited in Cochran-Smith and Lytle
1998: 26). He dismisses teacher research on the basis that understanding
events when one is a participant in them 'is excruciatingly difficult if not
impossible', thus negating the very possibility of the teacher functioning
as a researcher in his or her classroom setting. He suggests that, 'if there is
even the slightest possibility that the teacher can be a researcher, then the
"classic criteria" of qualitative research apply – that the teacher researcher
is bound by rules for the 'provision of evidence, consistency, freedom from
obvious bias, and perceptions of the people involved' (Huberman 1996,
cited in Cochran-Smith and Lytle 1998: 26) and must transcend the self in
order to transform an emic perspective into a 'more widely shared idiom'
(1996: 126). While granting that teachers have 'intimate local knowledge',
Huberman in effect undermines the value of this perspective by comment-
ing that accumulating and comparing teacher researchers' findings will keep
teacher researchers 'more honest', and that 'minimally reliable methods'
are needed to provide 'minimal safeguards against delusion and distortion'
(1996: 132). Hard and confrontational words indeed, and ones that provide little guidance at the level of practice or even politics.

Cochran-Smith and Lytle's (1998) view is quite different. They note the
paradoxical nature of teacher research as it is currently being implemented
in some contexts. They comment (1998: 21) that:

> the growth of the teacher research movement hinges on a paradox: as
> it is used in the service of more and more agendas and even institu-
> tionalized in certain contexts, it is in danger of becoming anything
> and everything. As we know however, anything and everything often
> lead in the end to nothing of consequence. It would be unfortunate
> indeed if the generative nature of teacher research contributed either
> to its marginalization and trivialization, on the one hand or its subtle
> cooptation or colonization on the other.

In this chapter, although I use examples and insights from my involvement in various teacher research projects, I am yet mindful of the paradox

and caution identified by Cochran-Smith and Lytle. I argue that teacher research has the potential to act as an important source of teacher and academic professional renewal and development because learning stands at the core of this renewal through the production and circulation of new knowledge about practice. The type of teacher research I have had experience with in various projects is collaborative in its application because the teacher researcher has not been working alone. This is in stark contrast to the type of work that Huberman seems to be referring to. My experience has been a collaborative enterprise in which teachers and academic colleagues work together, each providing different kinds of expertise and insight to the research project.

However, on the basis of my experience I suggest that teacher research is not without important warnings. Two issues provide the basis for my warnings. First, how do you overcome the cultural differences between school-based practitioners and academics to facilitate a climate of professional reciprocity? And second, whose research questions are investigated?

Before answering these questions I should first define some terms. I have used the terms 'practitioner research', 'collaborative enquiry' and 'action research' interchangeably but recognize that there are substantial differences between the three. Dadds and Hart (2001) provide a useful perspective on the differences between the various kinds of research methodology that come under the banner of teacher research, action research, practitioner research and so on. They argue:

> While there may be many characteristic differences in these several research methodologies (i.e. practitioner, action and teacher research), they share in common a central commitment to the study of one's own professional practice by the researcher himself or herself, with a view to improving that practice for the benefit of others.
>
> (Dadds and Hart 2001: 7)

It is this view of the development opportunity afforded by teacher research in whatever form that I take as given. Without such a focus, teacher research becomes reified and of little use to teachers individually or collectively.

For purposes of clarification in what follows, I briefly outline next the nature of teacher enquiry, action research and collaborative research, respectively.

School-based teacher enquiry

School-based teacher enquiry is primarily concerned with understanding and improving practice and can be seen as a way for teachers to know their own knowledge (Lytle and Cochran-Smith 1994), that is to make their knowledge explicit and problematical. Accordingly, it provides teachers with appropriate skills and practical possibilities to move beyond an unreflective and uncritical view and practice of professionalism. Carter and Halsall (1998: 73), writing from a school improvement perspective, identify some of the essential characteristics of this research. For them, teacher enquiry:

1 is grounded in data which has been systematically collected and analysed for a clearly defined purpose;
2 is undertaken by teachers, though sometimes with the support of external critical friends;
3 focuses on professional activity, usually in the workplace itself;
4 aims to clarify aspects of that activity, with a view to bringing about beneficial change – ultimately to improve student progress, achievement and development;
5 may focus on both teaching and learning at the classroom level, and supporting organizational conditions and change management capacity.

The primary aim of school-based teacher enquiry is twofold. First, it is concerned with understanding and improving practice; and second, it is a way for teachers to come to know the epistemological bases of their practice.

The Innovative Links project in particular has demonstrated how teacher enquiry provides teachers with opportunities to break with conventional wisdom about the nature of practice itself and in so doing provides opportunities for them to rethink how they can improve their practice. Moreover, there is clear evidence from this project that when teacher enquiry is complemented by academic research then new types of knowledge can be produced and new forms of teacher and teacher educator professionalism can be initiated. As Soltis (1994) observes, such projects provide teachers and academics with opportunities to develop a common language and multiple conceptual frameworks for exploring and reflecting upon what happens in classrooms.

School-based teacher enquiry creates opportunities for teachers and academics to develop new skills and in so doing it acts as a strong form of professional development for both groups. Among others, these opportunities include:

1 establishing and developing new roles (critical friend, resources person, sounding board, advocate etc);
2 establishing new structures (advisory groups, course-writing teams, paper-writing teams);
3 working on new tasks (proposal writing, documenting practices, curriculum planning, public presentations);
4 creating a culture of enquiry, whereby professional learning and dissemination are expected, sought after, rewarded and an integral and ongoing part of institutional and personal life.

Overall, teachers who have participated in teacher research projects like the NSN and Innovative Links did develop new skills: collecting and analysing data, publicly presenting their research to broader audiences, and developing a process which could be extrapolated across other areas of school improvement. Through the acquisition of such skills, teachers gained a clearer idea of their own and other's work practices. Whether or not this observation can be generalized across whole staff is uncertain. Certainly, reporting on research did help overcome problems of lack of cooperation from colleagues, because it documented individual and collective professional development and made it visible. This is an important point, for as Altrichter *et al.* (1993: 178) claim, 'in the long term, research knowledge developed by individual teachers can develop a collective knowledge base upon which individual members of the profession can draw and which will form a bond between them'. Indeed, when extrapolated to individual teachers and academic colleagues, opportunities may well arise for new forms of association and new practices for professional renewal will emerge.

Action research

Action research has often been the preferred methodology for teacher research because it aims to give teachers practical methods to develop knowledge from their experience and to make a contribution to the shared knowledge of the profession (Altrichter *et al.* 1993). Since it provides opportunities for building theories, it also facilitates teachers' overcoming some of the apprehension they have about theory and its role in helping them to understand their practice. Elliott (1991: 45) describes teachers' apprehension of theory:

> Teachers feel 'theory' is threatening because it is produced by a group of outsiders who can claim to be experts at generating valid knowledge about educational practices. Phenomenologically speaking, from the perspective of teachers, 'theory' is what researchers say about their practices after they have applied their special techniques of information processing. As such it is remote from their practice experience of the way things are. To bow to theory is to deny the validity of one's own experience-based craft knowledge.

Within school contexts, action research can be seen as a potent means of facilitating teacher involvement in change initiatives occurring in their own schools as well as validating teachers' theories in practice. This is an important issue because, as Schratz and Walker (1995: 107) argue, 'only theory can give us access to unexpected questions and ways of changing situations from within'. In the Innovative Links project, action research was viewed as one method for teacher enquiry because it provided a methodology for teachers to investigate and improve their practice in classrooms. Ideally, this type of research invites teachers to question the common assumption that knowledge for and about teaching should be primarily 'outside-in', that is, generated at the university and then used in schools (Lytle and Cochran-Smith 1994).

The experience of the NSN and the Innovative Links project has made it clear that the process of action research has enabled teachers to begin to ask critical questions about their practice and to undertake systematic means of enquiry in order to understand or improve their practice. It has also provided opportunity for teachers to theorize their work. The importance of this is captured by Ball (1995), who postulates the urgent role of theory as a way of 'thinking otherwise', a platform for 'outrageous hypothesis' and for 'unleashing criticism'. Theory, he claims, 'is destructive, disruptive, and violent. It offers a language for challenge and modes of thought, other than those articulated for us by dominant others' (Ball 1995: 266).

Paradoxically, however, while at one level this type of activity has enabled teachers to ask critical questions about their practice, in many cases such an approach has been less successful in allowing them to pose critical questions about the way their practice is politically defined or manipulated. Indeed, by focusing on practice, action research has come to the end of a long political process and in some ways has domesticated and limited the potential of the political and ideological analysis of change which an activist orientation to teacher professionalism is aiming to foster. Indeed, the importance of theory-generation from practice should not be underestimated.

Nevertheless, through the kind of systematic activity afforded by action research, professional conversations have emerged between groups of teachers and academics involved in research projects about the nature of practice and theory. Schratz and Walker (1995: 108) capture the nature of theory and its relation to practice and the changing of practice:

> Often we talk as though 'theory' were some kind of optional extra – a little used switch on the researcher's dashboard to be used, perhaps, only when driving on campus. Here we are suggesting quite the opposite – that theory is implicit in all human action.

The challenge for those working with teacher researchers is to recognize that there are two different forms of theory. One kind of theory takes its authority from the academy and the other kind is implicit in everyday life (Schratz and Walker 1995: 112). In our work in schools we need to acknowledge this and provide opportunities for the insights gained through understanding everyday life to filter into our daily practices in classrooms in schools and universities.

Collaborative enquiry

Collaborative enquiry is what occurs when teacher educators and practising teachers engage in processes of collaboration which articulate academic research and practitioner research. This articulation means that:

- teachers find out what is of value in the cross-contextual kind of research to their action research efforts, and accordingly can situate their reflective practice in a wider context of information and analysis of school reform;
- academic analysts not only become directly acquainted with what it means to be engaged in continuous improvement in teaching and learning in a specific context, but become aware of what teachers regard as important and relevant and why. This helps to ensure that when academic communication is oriented toward practitioners it is informed about the needs and requirements of practitioners and practice settings.

(Yeatman and Sachs 1995: 58)

Collaborative enquiry is neither simple nor easy. Because it makes new demands of both communities of researchers it necessarily assumes an experimental aspect. It is experimental in the kinds of social relationships developed, the degree of trust expected and the kinds of questions explored. This was certainly the experience of participants in the Innovative Links project. As a prime consideration for success of such endeavours it is important that neither partner asks the other to become the same as them. Instead each partner needs to come to respect and appreciate the difference between them and the different roles they play in the education enterprise.

This became evident during the reporting and documenting phases of the various projects. It should be clear that the demands of reporting and documenting are quite different depending on what type of research is in view. Action research, for example, demands different kinds of documenting and reporting from orthodox academic research. For the former, the kinds of documenting and reporting are likely to be intrinsic to the action cycle of continuous improvement. Within school-based contexts, the reporting of action research often belongs to relatively ephemeral types of communication represented in talk and dialogue. The reporting of academic research, on the other hand, is likely to take the form of formal talks or conference presentations, written publications and academic publications.

Whose questions get asked?

A central but unacknowledged dimension of school-based research, whether conducted by teachers and academics collaboratively or individually, is the issue of whose questions get put on the research agenda? This issue stands at the core of many successful or failed research attempts. If the research questions are posed by outsiders, in many cases academic researchers, then the research outcomes often have little effect on the classroom practices of teachers and the learning outcomes of students in schools. Alternatively, research that is undertaken on an equal basis between teachers and academics, where the research questions are posed collaboratively, can have a significant impact on classroom practice.

Typically, the type of research that is academic driven is communicated in a form that speaks to academic audiences rather than practitioner researcher ones. I am not suggesting that all school-based research needs to be addressed to practitioner and academic readers. Rather, I am suggesting that academics and practitioners need to negotiate the nature of the research and how it is to be published. If cultures of collegiality and professional reciprocity are to be valued and practised, then the groundrules for association must be negotiated, practised and then renegotiated. Pressures of time and the need to 'get the research out' often make this a difficult task. However, if the collaborative work is to continue then some of the taken-for-granted aspects of collaboration need to be made explicit. Goodwill, a commodity very often exploited in these types of research activities, may well run out and both academic researchers and practitioners will be the poorer for this failure. Indeed, it is often failure to recognize the different cultures of academic and practitioner researchers that creates tensions in this kind of research enterprise.

Acknowledging the different cultures

Following on from the observation above about different forms of reporting research, one of the warnings for academics and school-based practitioners working collaboratively is ensuring that each does not demand that the other becomes like him or her. This is particularly the case when issues about theory emerge. Professionally and experientially, school-based practitioners have different types of expertise from their university-based colleagues, and vice versa. At the core of these differences are quite distinct work practices and cultures. For academics, autonomy is a strong feature of their work practices and means that they have more control over their time than perhaps many of their school-based colleagues whose work practices are regulated more by bureaucratic and legal statutes. Another dimension of difference between the two are systems of reward. For academics it is demonstrated performance across teaching, research and administration/ service. Indeed, research performance, especially in terms of research grants, number and quality of publications and the ability to demonstrate the impact of the research are the measures of research performance that are rewarded. For teachers, the research dimension is not seen as a core feature of their performance.

At the core of developing the field of collaborative research between academics and teacher researchers is the idea of reciprocity, in particular recognizing that the work cultures, histories and expectations of teachers and academics are different. In my experience, many academics have worked hard to cross the divide between school and academic cultures, and their own experience in schools may have facilitated this. Many were sensitive to and conscious of the multiple demands being placed on teachers, and that in many cases, research projects were being done on top of already demanding professional lives. Unfortunately, in many cases the reciprocity, or the desire to cross the divide, was not demonstrated by teachers. They often showed disinterest in academic work or the demands that were placed on academics in their work. This may well be because, unlike the academics who 'knew' and had lived in a school culture, their school-based colleagues had experienced universities only as students. Understandably, their perceptions were of a power differential which may well block the possibility of a reciprocal gaze. Alternatively, they may genuinely not be interested in the academic culture, the workload and the multiple demands of teaching, research and administration which set limits, both in time and energy, to what academics might actually do with their teacher researcher colleagues. Nevertheless, the issue of recognition of the nature and constraints on the others' work is significant because it does help to create a more equal and generative climate. This is also crucial in the development of reciprocal cultures.

The theory/practice split stands at the core of the cultural differences between school and university staff. The view that experience counts and theory does not is a common comment when one engages in discussions with teachers. The words of a teacher involved in the Innovative Links project best present how one teacher responds to the theory/practice issue:

> Theory can sound OK and even be OK in practice but the crunch occurs at the chalk face – demands on teaching teams are enormous as teachers have to continue with all existing routines and responsibilities as well as assuming numerous NEW roles and responsibilities.

An ethic of practice which dominates teachers' orientation to their work often creates tensions between teachers and their academic colleagues when undertaking collaborative work. This pragmatic orientation emerges as a result of having to respond to multiple demands on their time and energy. I would suggest that it is the exigencies of classroom life that reinforce a pragmatic view rather than an anti-intellectual stance on the part of teachers. Again the words of a teacher reinforce this position:

> Academics tend to see things differently from teachers, who are usually too overworked to contemplate and reflect on their work. Their input is extremely valuable, but there is resistance towards them from some staff.

In this case it is the competing demands of working in schools that are seen to prevent teachers from researching and systematically documenting their practice. However, there is some equivocation by this teacher, who values seeing things differently herself, but who can also recognize that these different interpretations may not be appreciated by all of her colleagues. Nevertheless, this kind of work enables school-based practitioners to 'see anew' and to challenge the conventional wisdom of experience (Sachs 1997).

Not surprisingly, the idea of practice dominates teacher work. However, it became clear during the various Innovative Links projects and NSN work that, for many teachers, the distance and objectivity of the academic is seen to be a valuable resource. This is not least because the academic is differentially located, sociologically, politically and experientially, in the analysis of the politics and enactment of school change and reform. Understandably, the teacher immersed in the routine of classroom life does not necessarily have the interest, skills or time to be able to scrutinize political change either at the classroom or at the school level. This can be seen as one of the inherent problems of action and teacher research, and one of its more significant limitations.

Compounding the issue of the different cultures for academics is that often this type of work, namely teacher research, is not recognized by universities in terms of their reward structures. Working collaboratively with teachers, valuable as it might be for the renewing and enhancement of the profession and of individuals within it, does not fit with the externally imposed requirements of the ubiquitous research quantum and the documentation of research performance. In the current higher education climate in Australia and elsewhere, the assessment of research productivity as measured by research/publication output and successful competitive research grant bidding brings much-needed financial resources to faculties with diminishing resources. Furthermore, the intensification of the work of academics in universities often means that this kind of professional and scholarly engagement is done after all other responsibilities are dealt with.

On the basis of what I have presented above there are two tensions that need to be engaged with at a practical and at a strategic level. First is the ability of teachers to have the wherewithal to look behind the political assumptions that guide their work practices and the sorts of questions that this enables them to ask of themselves about that practice. Second is how collaborative research is acknowledged and supported by universities, in terms of both workload allocations and rewards, especially promotion.

Practitioner research and academic research

School research and university research serve different purposes; they have different tests for truth when evaluating the product of research and are inclined to approach methodological issues from different points of view. Put quite simply, teachers and teacher educators are likely to have different needs and requirements of research. For teachers, research will have as its main focus the improvement of practice, such as the examination of issues of immediate concern to a particular classroom or learning setting. Alternatively, academic research is concerned with validity and generalization. Academic research may be at the macro or the micro level; its primary concern is not the iterative feedback *for* improvement purposes but rather could be described as being oriented to the cross-contextual patterning of school efforts *at* improvement. Theirs is a research effort driven by the demand of cross-contextual or meta-analysis, not one driven by the demands of effective *doing* in the specific context in action (Yeatman and Sachs 1995).

To this end a distinction should be made between academic research and practitioner research. Indeed, while each serves different interests and purposes they can enrich the other, and should do so. However, when these two different types of research are lumped together under the generic category 'research' and their differences lost sight of, we are not able to enquire into this relationship of mutual enrichment, what it looks like and how it should work (Yeatman and Sachs 1995). If teachers come to see research as relevant to their practice, this is because the research is driven by the requirements of practice in specific contexts and its continuous improvement. In many cases this kind of research comes under the rubric of 'action research'.

Teacher educators as academic researchers may be involved with questions of improving practice in schools, especially as that practice relates to enhancing student learning outcomes. However, their research tends to be oriented to the cross-contextual patterning of such school efforts at improvement.

As Somekh (1994: 371) points out, the kinds of epistemological tests of these different kinds of knowing are quite different. For teachers, the value of action research resides in (1) how the ideas test out in practice and can be refined or modified through practice, and (2) the fit between their experimentation and what other teachers report of their experience.

The experience of the various projects in action made it quite clear that when there is a distinction made between academic and practitioner research it is then possible to focus attention on how these two types of research can be articulated, and for what purposes.

Documenting and reporting practitioner research

Teacher research provides teachers with the opportunity to make their knowledge public and to practise various forms of reflective dialogue. Given that, in many cases, substantial change and professional learning took place through teachers and academics alike, various vehicles need to be developed to disseminate the findings of the research to multiple audiences. Teachers' stories, or 'snapshots' of learnings, provide much needed detail on what is happening at the level of individual projects not only to participants but also to other interested parties. The publication of these stories has provided an impetus for more schools to get their stories out into the public domain.

The story of any project needs to be told so that others, inside and outside of the particular community, can have access to its achievements and learnings. The detail in which the story is told may vary, and the experience of the project confirmed this. In some cases it was detailed, full of rich descriptions of processes, procedures and outcomes; in others, information was provided in the form of brief accounts of successes and achievements. The work of the Western Melbourne Roundtable which was associated with the Innovative Links project is an exemplar of teachers writing about their practice. The writing developed as part of this project encouraged teachers to be self-reflective, not only about educational practice but also in relation to wider circumstances, constraints and opportunities in and beyond the workplace. The genre of the writing was that of case reporting, which were first-hand accounts written by practitioners who reported their practical experience.

Such writing can serve a variety of purposes within individual schools and across schools and systems. The purposes listed by the Western Melbourne Roundtable (1996: 13) included:

- To compile a public body of professional knowledge through descriptions of classroom practice.
- To explain the outcomes of teaching and learning through reflection on experience;
- To identify and generalise the underlying principles arising from individual events within classrooms;
- To provide a basis for the implementation of personal theories and strategies which lead to change and improvement in teaching and learning.

The experience of this project made it clear that documenting and reporting action research can take a variety of forms. However, it is important to note that what is learnt through the projects is extended beyond the participants and out into a broader professional and public domain. What the public domain is in any instance depends on the level of the project which is addressed. It can be more or less inclusive. However, the least inclusive level of documenting and reporting – the local public domain of the particular school as a learning community – is no less important than the more inclusive levels. The level of the public domain in each case needs to be addressed so that teachers find their own appropriate forms of making public their professional learning through various kinds of documentation and reporting.

Lessons learnt about teacher research

The examples of teacher research that I have drawn on in this chapter have given me cause to think about teacher research both as a strategy for renewing teacher professionalism and as a process to enhance the professional learning opportunities for teachers. Among the lessons learnt are the following:

1 First and foremost, the desire to engage in teacher research must be a choice, it cannot be mandated from the top down. Asking teachers to engage in time-consuming research when they are already struggling with multiple demands in their classrooms will not ensure success. More likely it will result in increased stress and a resistance to the benefits of research.
2 Teacher research should not be confused with academic research. These two types of research serve quite different purposes and have different tests of validity and reliability.
3 For teacher research to add the most value in terms of teacher professional learning it must be recognized as part of the workload of a teacher, it cannot be seen as an add-on.
4 Teachers engaging in research need support. This can come in a variety of ways. They can be supported and valued by the school leadership through the allocation of resources. Support can involve the establishment of networks of like-minded teachers who support each other and test ideas against each other. Finally, it can provide the vehicle for reciprocal learning for teachers and academics alike.
5 The limitations of the scope and outcomes of teacher research need to be acknowledged and the recognition made that teachers may not be in the best position to ask questions about practice when that practice may be circumscribed by state policy or education ideology.

Much can be learnt from the experience of teachers engaging in systematic enquiry into their practice. The major challenge is finding opportunities for teachers and others to talk about their experiences, the outcomes and the difficulties of engaging in this type of activity. This does not necessarily mean that the focus of such research is on 'what works'. Atkinson (2000: 328) captures the importance of educational research when she argues that 'the purpose of educational research is surely not to provide "answers" to the problems of the next decade or so, but to inform discussion among practitioners, researchers and policy-makers about the nature, purpose and content of the educational enterprise'.

Teacher research for professional renewal

There are many reasons for participating in teacher research. As indicated earlier, these include opportunities to promote change, to improve practice and student learning outcomes, and to contribute to knowledge construction which in turn enhances the status of teachers by formalising the knowledge base of the profession. There are two others that are closely intertwined: teacher research in collaboration with academic colleagues gives teachers and academics the opportunity to provide each other with an outsider's point of view. This in turn provides the basis for informal and ongoing professional renewal for both parties.

Maxine Greene (1995) observes that not being submerged in experience allows one to live more fully, more consciously, more aware of contingency, choice and the 'otherwiseness' of daily life. In a school context this could mean that one of the contributions an academic might make in a collaborative enterprise is to point out aspects of practice that teachers who are immersed in the hurly-burly that characterizes life in schools might overlook. Thus the potential to ask questions about the nature of practice and encouraging teachers to elaborate their perspectives or theories in action regarding their own and others' practice could provoke the emergence of new practices and opportunities. Furthermore, through prompting from outsiders, teachers can come to understand the political and ideological conditions which direct their practice in particular ways and towards particular ends. However, what should not be lost is taking advantage of opportunities for 'seeing anew' which emerge from both formal and informal conversations. The professional development opportunities for academics emerge as academics become involved in understanding the nature of life in schools. By engaging in collaborative work with teachers, academics' own 'theories' come to be debated and challenged. New forms of professional association emerge which, while on occasion challenging because of multiple demands being placed on academics, contribute to the overall project of teacher professionalism and enhance the status of the teaching profession. The strength and potential of these activities is, as Noffke (1997) points out, that knowledge is constructed collaboratively by teachers, students, administrators, parents and academics with the end of local developed curriculum and more equitable social relations. The contribution that action researchers make to knowledge is not narrowly technical, nor is it the production of 'findings', but rather the raising of fundamental questions about curriculum, teachers' roles, and the ends as well as the means of schooling. Furthermore, as Cochran-Smith and Lytle (1998: 32) argue:

> Like other efforts that interrupt the formal/practical and theory/ practice distinctions, this work challenges the very idea of a knowledge

base, and, drawing primarily on historical and political analyses, makes problematic some of the key concepts in discussions of teacher research, knowledge production and knowledge use.

The professional development potential of such activities lies not so much in the idea of skill development by either teachers or academics as in the opportunities that new forms of association provide (1) to disrupt previously taken-for-granted understandings of the world of practice and of the nature of knowledge in use, and (2) to raise questions about whose interests are served by the implementation of new policies and curriculum practices, what are the effects on and implications for teachers' work practices. As Cochran-Smith and Lytle (1998: 33) observe:

> teacher research can help to question and reinvent the whole idea of a knowledge base, disrupting the existing relationships of power among knowers and known – who decides what 'knowledge' and 'practice' mean? Who decides how knowledge ought to be interpreted and used in order to improve practice? Who decides what kinds of 'change' and 'improvement' are possible/desirable in schools and universities?

These important questions move the debate of teacher research and academic collaboration onto new levels. They move beyond traditional technical notions of professional development and create spaces for new kinds of conversations to emerge, different professional associations to be established and new discourses about schooling to develop. They provide opportunities for academics and school-based colleagues to be engaged in public critical dialogues and debates about the nature of practice and how it can be communicated with others and continually improved. Indeed they provide opportunities for what Goodson (1999) describes as the educational researcher as a public intellectual.

As suggested in the previous chapter, at the core of all of this is new forms of collaboration between teachers and academics. Soltis (1994: 255) puts it well:

> Genuine collaboration will not only require new teachers in new school cultures and structures, but also new teacher educators, new cultures in schools of education, and altered university structures for academics changing the culture and structure of the schools may look like a very difficult task, but not totally impossible.

The challenge, then, is to create the political and professional conditions where new cultures emerge and are sustained in schools and faculties of education where teacher research is rewarded and respected. At present this kind of research is seen to be at the margins of the research enterprise in universities.

Teacher research to support activist teacher professionalism

Through teacher research and collaboration with a variety of educational stakeholders the teaching profession develops a body of knowledge and information that not only helps to validate and affirm practice, but also contributes to the broader project of teacher professionalism. When this research has strong links between theory and practice and contributes to theory-building and knowledge application it becomes a fundamental strategy to support an activist teaching profession. Effective teacher research connects to the important issues that are facing teachers in their classrooms and helps them to understand the conditions that stand in the way of student learning. Such research also provides a systematic way for teachers to engage in ongoing conversations about their practice and to come to collaborative solutions that relate to issues of practice that they negotiate every day. Importantly, such collaborative and collegial work helps to break down the barriers of isolation and privatism. Classrooms are opened up for critical investigation, teachers' work practices are examined in order to understand and improve practice.

At its best, teacher research involves students in the research activity. Here another perspective is opened up for scrutiny. In this instance the teacher/student research nexus helps to create what David Hargreaves (1999) refers to as the knowledge-creating school. Such schools see the opportunities in and benefits of building a research capability which involves engaging students and teachers in research processes. They are also concerned with sharing methodologies which are appropriate for practitioner enquiry as a means for transforming teacher professional learning (Groundwater Smith 2001).

Teacher research should not be seen as an end in itself. It certainly has the potential to improve teachers' practice, it can provide opportunities for teacher professional renewal and most importantly can contribute to the larger political project of creating an activist teaching profession.

Conclusion

In this chapter I have drawn on my experiences working with teachers to undertake collaborative school-based research. My involvement with the NSN and the Innovative Links project have provided me with a variety of perspectives about the pleasures, potential and pitfalls of teacher research. Importantly, these projects have contributed as much to my own professional development as to that of the teachers with whom I worked. This kind of work prompted me to rethink whose questions get asked. Certainly, when I tried to impose my own research agenda on the activities I participated in with teachers, it became quite clear that my questions often had little relevance to the exigencies of classroom and school life. These interactions made me rethink the types of questions I posed, to reconsider the purposes of the research, both for myself and for the teachers, and finally, to re-evaluate issues of how teachers and academics can work collaboratively in the broader project of revitalizing the teaching profession.

Often, this kind of activity is seen as a significant form of *teacher* professional development, and it is. What I have been suggesting here is that teacher research undertaken in collaboration with academic colleagues is also a significant form of *academic* professional development. Seen as such, academics can learn a great deal which contributes to the broader goal of improving their own practice and also that of their students, many of whom will become the next generation of teachers. Furthermore, such activities have great potential to renew teacher professionalism and contribute to the broader political project of establishing a transformative teacher professionalism directed towards activist ends.

six

Transformative professionalism in practice

In the previous chapters I have been concerned with examining the versions of professionalism that dominate the theoretical literature and education policy discourse. I have also examined the broader political and social contexts that are shaping particular versions of professionalism in Australia and elsewhere. The purpose of this chapter is to provide examples of transformative professionalism in practice. The examples presented here are used to demonstrate the possibilities of a new teacher professionalism and are derived from large-scale professional development projects being undertaken Australia, the USA and Singapore. In Australia, the National Schools Network and the Innovative Links between Schools and Universities Project for Teacher Professional Development are examples of cross-system, national teacher professional development projects. In the USA the Coalition of Essential Schools is a principle-based approach to school reform. In Singapore, the Teachers' Network is a school-based teacher professional development initiative by the Ministry of Education.

All of these initiatives have as their central aim rethinking the taken-for-granted aspects of school and teachers' practice in order to improve student learning outcomes and student performance. Each of them in different ways proposes to construct new forms of schooling and new forms of professional engagement between teachers and other stakeholders through collaborative action. In all of these initiatives, teacher or practitioner research is a strategy used to look behind some current orthodoxies and to challenge the conventional wisdom of practice and experience. All of these projects embody democratic participation in schools in terms of the conceptualization and implementation of the projects. Finally, while each of the projects is responding to local needs and interests, the nature of classroom practice, the conditions under which most teachers work and the global imperatives being placed on education systems suggest that there are many similarities in how teachers are responding individually and collectively to various educational issues confronting them in the systems and schools in which they work.

In this chapter I argue that within the context of current educational reform agenda initiatives there are spaces which enable teachers to interrupt their taken-for-granted practices. Paradoxically, while many reform agenda initiatives have the possibility to deskill teachers through the intensification of their work, they have also provided new opportunities for teacher professional engagement or what was referred to earlier as transformative professionalism. Three questions shape this chapter:

1 How are these projects organized to develop a transformative teacher professionalism?
2 What do the projects have in common?
3 What do these projects tell us about teacher professional learning and transformative professionalism?

The projects described here represent a great amount of work, commitment and risk-taking on the part of teachers and other stakeholders. They represent new forms of work organization and networking, within and outside schools and with different stakeholders. Importantly, new forms of affiliation and respect have developed as a result of these projects. The vision and the hard work of all those involved in these projects can be described as no less than heroic. While important gains have been made by systems and teachers in terms of changing their individual practice by improving classroom student learning outcomes, it is important not to over-romanticize these projects. We must be aware that the work of these projects has not been taken up by the whole profession in Australia, the USA or Singapore. The answer as to why this is so is not simple; it has to do with the complex interplay of resources, funding, personal and professional disposition, and system and individual priorities. Nevertheless, these four examples do provide us with some models of what is possible if systems and teachers work together in the collective enterprise of renewing teacher professionalism.

Examples from the field

The four projects described in this chapter all have as one of their major goals improving student learning outcomes through teachers' rethinking their classroom practice. How this is achieved varies, as does how they are organized and their outcomes. The scope, funding and approaches to the development of a renewed teaching profession differ from country to country.

Nevertheless, what is common across all of these projects is the importance placed on teacher enquiry as a form of teacher professional development.

The National Schools Network

The Australian National Schools Network (NSN) and its precursor the National Schools Project (NSP) was conceived as a tool for system reform, and had the employers, unions, and Commonwealth government locked into supporting the process though the Teaching Accord of 1993. As Angus (1996: 145) observes, 'the primary target was not to enable improvement in the over 200 or so pilot schools, but rather to produce systemic changes that would enable the other 9800 schools in Australia to follow suit'.

Both the NSP and the NSN were action research projects designed to find out what was stopping schools from implementing their own ideas about improving teaching and learning. Conceptually, both projects operated from the following assumptions. First, the projects rejected the idea that there was one single recipe for school improvement and teacher professionalism. Second, it was recognized that if worthwhile changes were to occur, both the identification of the problem to be addressed by the change and the implementation of the prospective solution had to occur in the school community (Angus 1996). Finally, both projects were framed around the idea of work organization, that is the ways in which teachers' work was structured by organizational parameters, in particular those governed by government awards, industrial agreements, and so on. The NSN at its peak provided support for over 400 Australian schools that were rethinking their work organization and teaching and learning in order to improve learning outcomes for students and staff.

Organizationally, the NSN is a network of educational groups committed to improving teaching and learning for all Australian students. A National Coordinating Committee comprising representatives from education employing authorities, teacher organizations, and unions from the government and non-government sectors, teacher education representatives and the broader community, guides the organization.

Schools associated with the NSN focus their activities on two questions:

1 What is it about the way teachers work, in particular, the way they teach and organise their work, that gets in the way of student learning?
2 How can educators support each other to make the changes that are good for both learners and teachers?

These questions enable teachers in schools to challenge the orthodoxies of their practice, their taken-for-granted assumptions about their own and others' practice and to challenge traditional concepts and methods.

The work of the NSN[1] is informed by a set of nationally negotiated principles:

1 To be responsible for improving learning outcomes for all students.
2 To encourage greater student participation in the learning process.
3 To examine current work organization to identify good practice and impediments to effective teaching and learning.
4 To establish equality of access, opportunity and outcomes for all students.
5 To develop a model of participative workplace procedures and decision-making that includes the whole staff.
6 To understand industrial rights and responsibilities of all parties.
7 To encourage the whole community to be involved in decision-making about the reform process.

Ladwig and White (1996: 2) best sum up the work of the NSN. They comment that:

> [The] NSN is an Australian learning house of school reform knowledge and it supports member schools with ideas, professional development, electronic networking and research. Commitment to research is a key feature of the NSN's work, demonstrated in building a critical research culture in schools as an integral part of the rethinking process; and also in a substantial research program in partnership with university colleagues in order to evaluate progress towards NSN objectives. Its work in professional development focuses on organization critique and change.

To achieve its goals the NSN uses a variety of strategies, including teacher professional development programmes, conferences, training workshops which bring together educators from throughout Australia, and local-level workshops support for individual schools designed to help them re-examine their work.

Building a research culture is an integral aspect of the work of the NSN. Teachers, working collaboratively with university-based colleagues, parents, students or colleagues from employing authorities, have worked together on research projects of mutual interest. Ladwig and White (1996) argue that building a culture of research in member schools is an integral part of the rethinking process. 'Collegial critical reflective methodologies such as action research and case writing when integrated into rethinking processes, enable documentation and valid evaluation of the reforms at the school level as well as ownership and commitment' (1996: 4).

On the general level, most projects undertaken under the sponsorship of the NSN have been concerned with exploring effects of workplace restructuring. Where NSN schools develop their own contextualized reforms, the research projects aim to explore the impact of those reforms on pedagogy, student learning, teacher work organization, and school and organizational culture. The longer-term studies have had a wider focus examining the relationship between school restructuring and reform on the one hand and student learning outcomes on the other (Ladwig and White 1996).

Since 1993 the research programme of the NSN has explored the following issues:

- Changing curriculum and assessment structures.
- The links between restructure and organizational culture.
- Vertical school timetables and sub-school structures.
- The impact of key competencies on teacher work organization.
- Pedagogy and the introduction of new technologies.
- Teacher education and professional development.
- Leadership in reform contexts.

Teachers collaborating with university colleagues and other members of the profession have undertaken these projects in government and non-government schools. Funding to undertake the research has come from a variety of sources: the NSN itself, the federal government's Department of Education Employment, Training and Youth Affairs, grants from participating universities and, more recently, the corporate sector.

In what follows I present three examples of reform work being undertaken in schools which exemplify the diversity of ways in which teachers are rethinking their work practices. Teachers at Ascot Vale Primary School in metropolitan Melbourne, Victoria, have been concerned with reorganizing learning across the school through the implementation of 'mini schools'. The mini schools are organizational structures for regular teacher planning and review and professional development and delivery. The school subscribing to principles of collegiality adopted a two-team approach (Mini Schools One and Two) with a flat team structure. Team organization, planning and participation are essential elements of the structure and culture of the school.

As part of a dynamic form of work organization, teachers at Ascot Vale are not only concerned with the practice of teaching itself, that is working with children, but they are also constantly engaged in collaborative activities to develop team participation and skills at an individual, group and whole-school level. Team structures are organized for the purpose of planning and learning from each other, distributing the workload, so that teachers are able to use their time more efficiently and effectively in order to be in control of their own professional development.

As a result of their affiliation with the NSN and the work associated with this project, staff have refined new and existing teaching and learning strategies such as student-based curriculum planning, student contracts, group and individual enquiry learning, peer and cross-age tutoring that includes observation, shared experiences and reporting.

The project conducted at Ascot Vale has demonstrated the potential of collegiality, collaboration and time for focused conversations in promoting teacher professional learning. With the support of the NSN through allocation of resources and expertise, teachers in the schools developed a variety of new skills that helps to enhance their personal and professional knowledge bases. In particular they developed skills in systematic enquiry and the reporting of their findings to enhance the learning of colleagues within the school and at other schools. An important outcome of the project was that by documenting the learnings, that on many occasions were limited to those who were involved in the conversational aspects of the project, the findings of the project could be communicated to a wider audience of interested teachers. Making these learnings and the process of deliberation public and available to a wider audience, has opened discussions to more intensive critiques, so that the benefit of the experience has been expanded beyond the participants, to include the wider school community and the profession.

Bellambi Public School, a small primary school in regional New South Wales, is a school participating in the NSN which has been struggling with organizational structures. In this school the project took the form of creating both a learning community and a community of leaders. It has achieved this by adopting cooperative learning strategies among staff and expressing them through school decision-making.

The project undertaken at Bellambi represents a major departure from traditional structures, both administrative and organizational. As a result it has required a profound reculturing of the school and its communities. Rethinking leadership so that there is shared responsibility for decision-making has provided a substantial challenge for the hierarchical and line management ethos of New South Wales schools. Collegiality is essential to the working of the school. The new structures developed and the resources to sustain the change are devoted to enabling learning between staff to take place. Two related consequences of the project are that the traditional isolation of teachers in classrooms and the privacy of those classrooms are breaking down.

The project at Bellambi Primary School was concerned with restructuring and reculturing the school. The cumulative effect has been to alter attitudes and behaviours at all levels of the school community. Currie and Groundwater-Smith (1998: 11–12) describe the changes as the following:

Structural change
- School management plan developed by the whole staff;
- One school rather than separate primary and infants departments;
- Joint decision-making by all paid workers in the school;
- Professional development undertaken, where possible by teams not individuals;

- Executive work not based upon traditional responsibilities;
- Ongoing whole-school activities organized through vertical group-
  ings;
- Learning programs for parents;
- Changed classroom practices and organization as a result of Coop-
  erative Learning and Action Research;
- School structured to allow for collegial support during school time.

Cultural change
- Increased emphasis on staff development;
- Professional development largely internally driven and resourced;
- All staff responsible for school discipline;
- Executive role one of coaching/mentoring rather than supervision;
- Philosophy of cooperative learning – strongly encouraging adults as
  learners and teachers as researchers;
- Peer tutoring, joint planning and co-researching among staff;
- Legitimation of risk taking and change among staff.

A notable outcome of the project at Bellambi Primary School was that
the development of cooperative learning created a higher degree of professional collaboration among teachers. Additionally, teachers and students
work closely together to negotiate learning situations. Students are actively
encouraged to work together to share knowledge and understanding (Currie
and Groundwater Smith 1998).

Other important benefits of the project identified by Currie and Groundwater Smith (1998: 20–1) include:

- Increased teacher confidence in understanding the teaching and learn-
  ing process and their own classroom practice;
- Increased teacher and parent confidence in charting the educational
  course for the school through considered inquiry;
- Development of a whole school focus and commitment to a shared
  vision for teaching and learning;
- Greater emphasis upon community relations and improved parent
  involvement;
- Increased student confidence;
- Greater adaptability to and acceptance of change by students and
  staff;
- Confidence in publicly disclosing school practice to both celebrate,
  learn and reflect upon them.

The costs of undertaking a project like this are best summed up by the
principal: 'People need to know that this model (management by empower-
ment and cooperative learning) is not cost free and is energy depleting.'
(Currie and Groundwater Smith 1998: 21).

In both Ascot Vale and Bellambi the intention has been to rethink management and classroom practices so that the emphasis is away from managing and redirected to learning. Not surprisingly this has created some challenges for teachers working in a new structure. The changes have meant that much of the conventional wisdom and many of the taken-for-granted practices of teachers in classrooms have been challenged, in particular what it means to be a teacher and how learning is organized. The outcomes of these two projects, namely flatter management structures, an authentic culture of cooperation, a learning environment that is more productive in terms of students' learning and teacher satisfaction, and community involvement, all attest to the mutual benefits gained from projects that were seen at the beginning to be high risk.

The third example describes a joint project between NSN and the Australian Curriculum Studies Association (ACSA) in the development of resources and materials in the area of middle schooling and an integrated curriculum. In this project, seven NSN schools worked to develop various kinds of materials – print and video, overview paper, school outlines and samples of work – to provide various entry points to explore an integrated curriculum in the middle years of schooling in Australia. To participate in the project, schools had to submit a proposal which was then reviewed. Inevitably, the experience of doing the projects meant that some adjustments had to be made from the original submission.

In the seven schools that participated there were wide-ranging definitions and practices of an integrated curriculum, sometimes within one school. There was no single approach to middle schooling, or towards an integrated curriculum across these schools, although there were clear shared principles about what counts as important in the curriculum and how this might be best organized to facilitate improved student learning outcomes (Brennan and Sachs 1998).

The schools participating in the project represented a wide variety of locations and type, including metropolitan and rural, new and established, government and independent across three states and the Australian Capital Territory.

One of the major research findings of this project is the systematic approach which links curriculum and organization, affecting all parts of the school's efforts with these students. It is the integration of effort, not only integration of curriculum, across different dimensions of school organization that is central. What is noteworthy here are the links that emerge for any change process involving school architecture, school change arrangements, staff organization, approaches to learning, teaching and assessment, and professional development through ongoing research (Brennan and Sachs 1998: 12).

In each of the participating schools, integrated projects are used as a focus for the overall organization of the middle years but with some additional time on specific subject or skills areas. Some use 'principal' or 'home room' teachers as the organizing focus for students and curriculum alike. Others teach in small teams, whereas yet others plan together but teach separately (Brennan and Sachs 1998).

Of the schools involved in this project, four models relating to the types of school, their organizational structure and the approach to middle schooling and integration were identified:

1 *New schools with different organizational structures.* Two schools established a different approach to curriculum and school structure from their very inception. Lanyon High School in the Australian Capital Territory and The Grange Secondary College in Victoria established middle schooling structures in grades 7 and 8, characterized by small teaching teams and curriculum clusters which followed through as the schools grew.
2 *Existing schools with multidisciplinary teaching teams.* Three schools (Kurri Kurri and Vincentia High Schools in NSW and Eumemmering Secondary College in Victoria) introduced year-level integrated classes taught by small teams that span several key learning areas. In at least one school, double classrooms form the 'home room' of that class.
3 *Integration through the use of technology.* St Aidan's, an independent girls' school in Queensland, offered a different approach to integration through the use of technology, specifically in the development of the use of an intranet (a local Internet facility) as a tool to access and publish student work.
4 *Whole-school approach.* At Oatlands School in rural Tasmania the focus of the project was on care. In this school, welfare and behaviour management were closely integrated with an approach to curriculum which centred on consistent and shared pedagogy.

In each of these schools, teacher practice, classroom organization, curriculum materials and school ethos have had to alter significantly from the norm that has been taken for granted: schools with classes separately taught for each discipline, assessed separately, and planned and delivered by teachers in isolation. In undertaking these initiatives, Brennan and Sachs (1998: 20) note that changes have had to be made to:

1 the practice of curriculum;
2 school organization and facilities;
3 making students partners in curriculum deliberations;
4 teacher planning and teamwork;
5 social relations and technologies of change.

The Australian materials produced from this project made an important contribution to curriculum debate and to research and practice in school change efforts in general and middle schooling in particular. The emerging findings from this project confirm Australian and American research on the problems associated with students in the middle years of school. Furthermore, they provide practical solutions to a variety of problems experienced by teachers and students in schools.

The emerging findings vary across schools, depending in part on how long the initiatives have been in place. In those with longer-term projects, there is evidence of literacy gains in achievement across a range of students. Students are spending more time on their academic work, a particularly useful outcome for those who truant regularly. Significantly, drops in rates of truancy and levels of violence in schools were reported in most of the schools along with increased social skills in dealing with conflict. Increased capacities for cooperation by both students and teachers, especially on research projects, was noted, as was increased efforts by students to use libraries and new technologies in complex ways (Brennan and Sachs 1998).

In the three examples presented here, NSN schools have developed projects that have been concerned with asking teachers to examine and question the link between the organization of teachers' work and pedagogy. The NSN continually links teacher professional development with ongoing school-based research initiatives. The NSN research framework involves building a research culture among teachers in schools. Furthermore, it promotes and supports collaborative research and collegial reflective practices using critical action research methodologies.

Through such an orientation to school practice, teachers in schools are actively concerned with changing various aspects of their own practice. Through these projects, teacher professionalism is being redefined from within the profession rather than from outside. These projects strongly confirm the possibility of a transformative teacher professionalism.

Innovative Links between Schools and Universities Project for Teacher Professional Development

The Innovative Links project is another example of a nationwide initiative that challenges established conceptions as to what schooling, teacher professionalism and teacher education is about. It complements and builds upon the experience of NSN. This is not by chance. Key academics were members of an NSN academic reference group which asked specific questions about the relationship between research and practice in the work of teachers. Conceptually and organizationally, then, the Innovative Links project was built upon the procedures, learnings and principles of participation established through the NSN (and its predecessor, the NSP). As part of the discussion, a new and reciprocal element emerged about the relationship between research and practice in the work of university academics in the field of teacher education. It has been designed to move participants beyond their accustomed ways of doing things and their familiar relationships (Yeatman and Sachs 1995).

During its operation from 1994 to 1996, the Innovative Links project provided the opportunity for 14 universities, across 16 campuses, representing all Australian states and one territory to be involved in a project that had as its core feature the idea of partnerships between practising teachers on a whole-school basis and university-based teacher educators. This was approximately one-third of universities in Australia involved in a coherent teacher professional development project. Added to this were some 100 schools which included state, independent, Catholic representatives and some 80 academic associates. Three million dollars were allocated over three years to support the project. This was the first time that such substantial resources were allocated for a national teacher professional development project.

The Innovative Links project represented formal and explicit partnerships between schools and universities which were seen as central to the renewal and development of teacher professionalism; this was enabled by the formation of local roundtables comprising five or six schools and academic associates from the affiliated university. As Yeatman and Sachs (1995) observed, for the first time the relationship between teacher education faculties in universities and schools had come onto the school reform/restructuring agenda in Australia. The project focused on the question of how this relationship should be designed and developed to facilitate the professional development of both school- and university-based practitioners. The basic premise upon which Innovative Links and NSN were formulated is the construction of a learning community. In the context of schooling, teachers can be regarded as providing the leadership and facilitation of processes whereby students learn the skills and knowledge which enable them to take responsibility for their own learning. Within such a context, student learning is only one of the dimensions. Teacher learning must be incorporated, as must academic learning and systems learning, if the idea of a learning community is to be fully realized (Yeatman and Sachs 1995).

Projects supported through Innovative Links were conducted in primary and secondary schools, in urban, suburban, rural and remote locations. Kelso High School, for example, is a high school located on the eastern edge of Bathurst, a rural town in western New South Wales. The Charles Sturt University Roundtable coordinated the project. According to the principal of the school, the Innovative Links project provided 'a lubricant for change'. The Innovative Links project gave the school a mechanism and the time and resources to boost innovative teaching and learning in specific faculties. The project has enabled 'the creation of a climate where change is seen as acceptable to the majority of the school community. From the point of view of outside observers, the change has been positive and dynamic. The ideas, structures and dialogue generated have the potential not only to change the school, but to flow onto wider educational audiences' (Currie *et al.* 1996: 33).

The project at Kelso High School focused on developing diagnostic and remediation programmes in mathematics. An important feature was the association of the school with Charles Sturt University and Raglan Primary School, the latter being one of Kelso High School's local feeder schools. The dialogue and interaction between these three groups enabled participants to come to understand the huge changes in teaching and learning practices in primary schools, which are often not reflected in secondary classrooms.

Currie *et al.* (1996) describe the project in the following terms. In 1995, an innovative alternative organizational structure was implemented for year 7 – the block structure. Year 7 students were placed in one of three blocks, with each subject timetabled together. Each block contained students with a range of abilities. This timetabling structure allowed:

1 students to be grouped in different ways, giving scope for mixed-ability classes, streamed classes or specific groupings such as gifted and talented, remedial, gender, experience or other criteria;
2 teachers to work collaboratively, especially within a subject area;
3 student welfare needs to be met through a year adviser and two year 7 assistants, each having responsibility for students within a block.

The project was continually monitored and evaluated by teachers within the school. According to one of the teachers, 'There was more discussion and talk among and between teachers, more sharing of ideas, more collaborative teaching practices and, among some teachers, a change in teaching and learning strategies' (quoted in Currie *et al.* 1996: 35).

The success of the maths project had a cascading effect across other subject areas in the school. The science faculty started a learning centre modelled on the numeracy one set up earlier by the mathematics faculty. The aim was to develop independent learners and to focus on 'able' and gifted and talented students. Here students were involved in problem-solving activities and negotiated criteria for this work with their teachers and peers. This proved to be a powerful motivator in engaging students in the learning process: 'I love Science because I am in charge of my own outcomes', enthused one year 8 student at Kelso High School (quoted in Currie *et al.* 1996).

In the English faculty, teachers were also involved in actively changing work practices. The need for clear outcomes in each unit of work in years 7 and 8 became a prime focus. These teachers examined the cooperative learning focus, which is central to the block structure, from a different perspective. By starting with year 7 and 8 exit outcomes, the English staff found alternative ways of expressing outcomes to parents, students and staff. One consequence of this, reported by Currie *et al.* (1996), was that 'staff were noticing that they were talking to each other more about their work'.

The project at Kelso High School indicated the importance of teachers in primary and secondary schools talking to each other about pedagogy, teaching strategies and curriculum content. It also facilitated opportunities for teachers to engage with each other in dialogue about the nature of their work and how they structured and evaluated student learning. Finally, it provided a significant change in organizational structures within the school, especially as they related to timetabling.

The second project was undertaken by the Northern Territory University Roundtable. This project was undertaken in a remote area Aboriginal school, Yirrkala Homeland School, and involved a cluster of schools operating in the Homeland Centre communities of North-East Arnhem Land, namely Baniyala, Biranybirany, Boruwuy, Dhalinybuy, Gurrumuru, Gutjangan, Garrthalala and Gangan.

The Homeland Centre-based schools that constitute the Yirrkala Homeland School are staffed by Yolngu Homeland Centre teachers, who are employed by the Northern Territory Department of Education as assistant teachers. Eight teaching staff employed as visiting teachers and who are based at Yirrkala Homeland School's Education Resource Centre, support these teachers. These groups of teachers, who are generally separated by great distances, work together in professional development activities related to curriculum development and the implementation and evaluation of appropriate curriculum for Homeland Centre-based students. The project at Yirrkala Homeland School was focused on improving the teaching and learning of English (Grenfell and Clancy 1998).

The objectives of this project were:

1 To improve the collective teaching practice of Yirrkala Homeland School teaching staff while maintaining and strengthening Yolngu[2] control and participation in the teaching/learning programmes.
2 To explore ways of adapting available materials to make productive contribution to the educational processes.

The project enabled teachers in the school to explore the nature of the difficult educational context in which the curriculum would be developed, implemented and evaluated. In the context of the Yirrkala Homeland School, these difficulties related to:

1 the cross-cultural situation;
2 geographical isolation;
3 the multi-grade nature of the sites involved.

Grenfell and Clancy (1998) argue that the Innovative Links project sought to explore ways that existing resources could be effectively and efficiently used. The resources included the participants themselves, community members, teachers and staff of the Yirrkala Community Education Centre, Northern Territory Department of Education staff, telecommunications, information technologies and existing computer hardware and software.

The project developed from the recognition that both professional and curriculum development are integral elements of any attempts to achieve improved learning outcomes. The problem faced by this Innovative Links project team was how to increase and improve the quality of support for Homeland Centre-based Yolngu teachers and focus on the English language programme in order to improve educational outcomes in Homeland School (Grenfell and Clancy 1998).

The major task related to visiting teachers examining their practice in relation to how they assisted in improving Homeland Centre teachers' confidence and competency in English. Recognition that the Homeland Centre teachers are the primary educators of the Homeland Centre-based students was paramount. Active respect for the skills that the Homeland Centre teachers bring to the teaching situation, as well as the teaching situation itself, could all be lost in the drive to improve the English knowledge of these students. The task facing the Innovative Links project team required all participants to adopt the slogan of 'we are all learners' in the process of developing the English language programme (Grenfell and Clancy 1998: 52).

The action research approach adopted in the project informed, linked and integrated staff professional development with the process of changing and improving curriculum. The action research approach described by Grenfell and Clancy (1998) consisted of a six-phase cycle: identifying the problem or difficulties; taking action; recording observations relating to the actions; reflection; replanning; and recommencing the cycle.

Grenfell and Clancy (1998: 59) observe that as a result of students and staff participating in this project, the following changes in workplace practice have occurred:

1 Participating staff developed ways to maintain records of the learning journey to show the successes and difficulties experienced which are used to inform the English programme's planning cycle.
2 Students across the Yirrkala Homeland School work in groups that share common learning experiences and learning materials as a way to ensure that these minimal requirements are addressed in each learning cycle.
3 All teachers at Yirrkala Homeland School attend regular professional development and curriculum development workshops. Currently these workshops facilitate a way for participating Homeland Centre teachers to work towards the achievement of course outcomes for the Batchelor College General Education Program.

4 Participation in the General Education Program requires ongoing exploration of a range of issues related to recognition of workplace-learning and the requirement for service delivery institutions to have the flexibility to fully exploit the possibilities of workplace learning in providing appropriate and relevant training and professional development.

The action research project helped teachers to rethink their practice. It also provided opportunities for teachers to meet in order to share, reflect on and plan units of work collaboratively. Thus, existing links between staff in all schools were strengthened and new ones developed. These links provided opportunities to take the schools in new directions in terms of planning, practice, community involvement and teacher professional development.

Both the NSN and the Innovative Links project have been concerned with revitalizing schools and teacher professionalism through teacher learning. Both projects emphasized processes of enquiry, a collaborative work context, and improving student and teacher work conditions and learning outcomes. The schools associated with both projects encouraged teachers to understand and engage in the minds of learners, and to devise strategies, individually and collectively, which will improve students' learning outcomes.

Teachers working in NSN and Innovative Links schools developed skills and competencies to undertake classroom-based action research into dilemmas of teaching, such as investigating problematic aspects of the curriculum, attempting to understand learners' conceptions of subject matter content, examining difficult student behaviour and many other demanding aspects of classroom and school life. The collaboration between the schools and university academics has led to field-based teacher research and to the development of different kinds of relationships (professional and social) between the two parties concerned with teacher preparation and development.

Importantly, both of these projects have been concerned with developing what Lave and Wenger (1991) refer to as communities of practice. They argue that social practice – what practitioners do and how they talk about what they do – is the primary generative phenomenon, and learning is one of its characteristics. They locate 'learning not in the acquisition of structure, but in the increased access of learners to participating roles in expert performance' (Lave and Wenger 1991: 17). Learning is thus a way of *being* in a particular social world not merely knowing about it or describing it. From this perspective, emphasis is placed upon participation in a community of practitioners, rather than merely the acquisition of a set of skills or practices deemed to satisfy bureaucratic requirements. Through their involvement in the NSN and the Innovative Links project, teachers and academic colleagues move from peripheral involvement to one of full participation. This process provokes and facilitates a conversation about learning, and about how people can learn from projects and each other. This conversation becomes an ongoing aspect of school life, an important source of knowledge for the development of professional practice.

An indicator of the success of the Innovative Links project is the determination of a number of roundtables to continue their work in spite of the cessation of external funding. In these instances the principles of affiliation and involvement in teacher professional development have become embedded in the structures and processes of both schools and universities. However, it must also be stated that this did not occur in all roundtables. The success of these projects lies in terms of the extent to which the work and outcomes of projects were embedded into the everyday work practices of teachers and the organizational structures of schools. The lasting effects are yet to be documented.

The Coalition of Essential Schools

The work of the Coalition of Essential Schools (CES) provided much of the conceptual framework for the two projects described above. Like the NSN and the Innovative Links project, the CES is a school reform initiative aimed at improving student achievement. The CES is a grassroots reform network which, in 2001, comprised 1200 schools and 20 regional centres across the USA and abroad. The work of CES is to be found in urban, suburban and rural schools. Ninety-seven per cent of schools associated with CES are public (i.e. state) schools. CES represents the vision of Ted Sizer as elaborated in his 1984 landmark book *Horace's Compromise*.

The work of CES schools is premised on the Coalition's Common Principles which articulate a vision of education where students are active learners and are able to demonstrate skills and knowledge publicly; in which teachers tune instruction to individual needs and design curricula to promote deep understanding rather than mere coverage of material; and in which school schedules and routines help teachers and students to know each other well and to work in an atmosphere of trust and high expectations. (Simon and Gerstein n.d.).

In order to gain membership into the CES,[3] schools must subscribe to all or most of the following ten principles:

- The school should focus on helping young people learn to use their minds well. Schools should not be comprehensive if such a claim is made at the expense of the school's central intellectual purpose.
- The school's goals should be simple: that each student master a limited number of essential skills and areas of knowledge. While these skills and areas will, to varying degrees, reflect the traditional academic disciplines, the program's design should be shaped by the

intellectual and imaginative powers and competencies that the students need, rather than by 'subjects' as conventionally defined. The aphorism 'less is more' should dominate: curricular decisions should be guided by the aim of thorough student mastery and achievement rather than by an effort to merely cover content.

- The school's goals should apply to all students, while the means to these goals will vary as those students themselves vary. School practice should be tailor-made to meet the needs of every group or class of students.

- Teaching and learning should be personalized to the maximum feasible extent. Efforts should be directed toward a goal that no teacher have direct responsibility for more than 80 students in the high school and middle school and no more than 20 in the elementary school. To capitalize on this personalization, decisions about the details of the course of study, the use of teaching materials and specific pedagogies must be unreservedly placed in the hands of the principal and staff.

- The governing practical metaphor of the school should be student-as-worker, rather than the more familiar metaphor of teacher-as-deliverer-of-instructional-services. Accordingly, a prominent pedagogy will be coaching, to provoke students to learn how to learn and thus to teach themselves.

- Teaching and learning should be documented and assessed with tools based on student performance of real tasks. Students not yet at appropriate levels of competence should be provided with intensive support and resources to assist them quickly to meet those standards. Multiple forms of evidence, ranging from ongoing observation of the learner to completion of specific projects, should be used to better understand the learner's strengths and needs, and to plan for further assistance. Students should have opportunities to exhibit their expertise before family and community. The diploma should be awarded upon a successful final demonstration of mastery for graduation – an 'Exhibition.' As the diploma is awarded when strict age grading and with no system of credits earned by 'time spent' in class. The emphasis is on the students' demonstration that they can do important things.

- The tone of the school should explicitly and self-consciously stress values of unanxious expectation ('I won't threaten you but I expect much of you'), of trust (until abused) and of decency (the values of fairness, generosity and tolerance). Incentives appropriate to the school's particular students and teachers should be emphasized. Parents should be key collaborators and vital members of the school community.

- The principal and teachers should perceive themselves as generalists first (teachers and scholars in general education) and specialists second (experts in but one particular discipline). Staff should expect multiple obligations (teacher–counsellor–manager) and a sense of commitment to the entire school.
- Ultimate administrative and budget targets should include, in addition to total student loads per teacher of 80 or fewer pupils on the high school and middle school levels and 20 or fewer on the elementary level, substantial time for collective planning by teachers, competitive salaries for staff, and an ultimate per pupil cost not to exceed that at traditional schools by more than 10 percent. To accomplish this, administrative plans may have to show the phased reduction or elimination of some services now provided students in many traditional schools.
- The school should demonstrate non-discriminatory and inclusive policies, practices, and pedagogies. It should model democratic practices that involve all who are directly affected by the school. The school should honor diversity and build on the strength of its communities, deliberately and explicitly challenging all forms of inequity.

(CES website www.essentialschools.org)

These common principles provide coherence across all coalition schools. According to Simon and Gerstein (n.d.: 3):

> the principle based approach assumes that rather than being 'implementors', teachers, administrators and community members are, in fact 'inventors'. It assumes that good schools must be finely attuned to their students and to their local needs and resources. The Faculty and community of a CES school must decide how to apply the principles in its school's unique context, for the principles assert powerful ideas about schooling rather than mandating particular action.

Significantly, the common principles do not assert a blueprint for change but rather challenge a school community to examine its priorities and to redesign the curriculum, instruction, assessment and organizational structures (Simon and Gerstein n.d.). Indeed, while there are similarities in school projects and the strategies that are devised to respond to local issues, CES does not prescribe a model; rather, a set of principles provides the basis for all the work of CES schools. Importantly, schools do not work in isolation; they borrow from each other. This collaborative or problem-solving approach enables sustained discussions between various groups interested in educational reform about what common practices and issues might mean and how various communities might assist each other in finding their best solution.

Like the NSN and Innovative Links, the CES utilizes a variety of strategies to facilitate its work at both national and school levels. Regional centres support schools in the process of change by facilitating learning among schools in the region and by providing carefully targeted opportunities for professional development and technical assistance. Like the projects themselves, CES regional centres vary in their areas of focus but are all guided by the common principles and similar strategies.

The work of CES is to provide support to schools in four areas: school design, classroom practice, leadership and community connections. CES's programme in school design is guided by principles that the school's rigorous intellectual goals must apply to all students and that each student is known well, that the school models democratic practices and strives for equitable outcomes, that school community resources are directed to focus on the school's intellectual purpose, and that diplomas are awarded on the basis of mastery (CES website www.essentialschools.org).

Initiatives concerning classroom practice are based on the assumption that the teacher's role is not merely the transmission of information, but rather to foster student enquiry and the development and practice of skills. The curriculum should emphasize thoroughness and depth over breadth of coverage, with an aim of developing habits of mind such as enquiring into causes, seeing from multiple perspectives, and applying learning to new situations. The curriculum should be flexible and individualized enough to allow for independent exploration. Students who do not meet stated standards should be given intensive support so that they can meet those standards.

CES provides a variety of strategies to help teachers in the area of classroom practice. Some strategies include: teacher collaboration and enquiry groups to act as critical friends or coaches; visits to like-minded schools; peer coaching training; and CES university courses such as 'Inquiry based instruction', 'Teacher research' and 'How to personalize instruction'.

Support to enhance leadership takes a variety of forms. The programme in leadership is premised on the following assumptions: that leading a school well demands high formal leadership and collaboration at every level; a key role of those in leadership positions is to support ongoing improvement in the instructional practices of staff and to keep the school focused on its intellectual mission; leadership structures and decision-making procedures should model democratic practices and should communicate a tone of high expectations and trust (CES website www.essentialschools.org).

Community connections are an important aspect of CES work. The assumption is that learning takes place inside and outside of the school, and can be supported by community members mentoring and contributing to the intellectual life of the school.

Schools associated with CES have reported various positive outcomes. For example, evidence reported from Northport High School in Michigan indicated greater teacher communication across faculties and a sense of collegiality; this was based on teachers reflecting on what had changed and what had remained the same in their practice and work environment since the reform was initiated. Teachers also reported as sense of autonomy in controlling the reform initiative as a CES school, compared with the experiences as a non-CES school (Lockwood 1998). Importantly, 95 per cent of CES schools involved teachers in decision-making compared with the national average of 52 per cent (Simon and Gerstein n.d.).

Other evidence has suggested that student discipline problems have been reduced. Research into CES schools between 1997 and 2000 found that, after joining the Coalition, schools reported a 50 per cent decrease in discipline referrals and fewer incidents of violence.

Gerstein (1999) reports that there have also been differences between student outcomes in CES and non-CES schools. Differences have been identified in standardized tests in literacy and maths. SAT (student achievement test) scores in CES schools have been significantly higher than those in non-CES schools. The US average for SAT scores is 1015 whereas the average for CES schools is 1048.

Collegial networks and ongoing professional development of teachers have also been positive features of CES work. Exhibitions Collections showcase the assessment designs and practices that CES teachers have implemented, either on the web or at regional conferences and workshops. These provide classroom-based examples of why an initiative worked or why it failed, providing relevant material for other teachers in the network.

CES teachers are reported to 'actively' pursue ongoing training and collegial support, conduct action research and collaborate to develop innovative curriculum and teaching practices. Working in a CES school gives teachers opportunities to interact with colleagues from other schools and other disciplines. Professional conversations about practice are fostered, and collective solutions to individual problems and issues are discussed. Teachers learning from each other are fostered in an environment of trust and collegiality. Here a transformative professionalism contributes to the development of an activist teaching profession.

The Teachers' Network

The Teachers' Network (TN) is a Singapore Ministry of Education-sponsored network of teachers across primary and secondary schools in Singapore which was established in April 1998. Its mission as set out on its website is to 'serve as a catalyst and support for teacher-initiated development through sharing, collaboration and reflection leading to self-mastery, excellent practice and fulfilment'. While different from the projects in Australia and the USA, in that TN is a ministry-sponsored initiative, it does have as its focus enhanced teacher professionalism, albeit of a particular kind, and a research-based form of teacher professional development.

The work of TN is based on four beliefs: reflection, self-mastery, excellent practice and fulfilment. These beliefs reinforce and complement one another and develop both personal and professional qualities in teachers. Reflection is understood to be the key to meaningful learning. It generates new ideas, transforms minds and hearts and engenders growth. Self-mastery is to grow in personal effectiveness. TN provides teachers with opportunities to grow as people and as professionals. Excellent practice stands at the core of teachers' professional competency and is achieved through critical examination of pedagogy and classroom practice. Teachers engaging in a variety of strategies achieve excellent practice and techniques aimed at improving student learning. It requires that teachers continuously upgrade their content and pedagogical knowledge as well as skills. Fulfilment is the job satisfaction enjoyed by teachers as a result of enhanced competency and confidence and the conviction that teachers mould the future of the nation.

A variety of strategies are utilized by those associated with TN to achieve its mission. These include acting as catalysts, providing support, facilitating teacher initiatives and encouraging collaboration.

The TN provides resources for teachers in schools to participate in school-based professional development. By providing support to teachers, those teachers are actively encouraged to engage in innovative practices in a context where risk-taking is encouraged and enquiry into practice is expected. Advisory staff from the TN work with teachers who have generated 'good ideas' that relate to their own practice. These ideas are then worked through and their results are shared with peers and colleagues in their own and other schools.

Many of these ideas are communicated over the Internet through chatrooms or the TN website. Teachers can hold online discussions on topics of mutual interest. To date, the use of chatrooms by teachers has not been fully realized. It would appear that teachers prefer face-to-face interaction at present. Discussion topics include curriculum issues, classroom management, teaching materials and resources, and various teaching strategies and tips.

An important feature of the work of TN is that many of its activities are generated and run by teachers themselves. For example, teachers working in schools run numeracy skills workshops on particular aspects of classroom practice or in other curriculum areas such as literacy. Here the expertise of teachers is recognized and the importance of teachers learning from each other is reinforced.

Research into practice is encouraged and supported by the TN. Action research has been used by many teachers to examine an issue that is of interest or importance to them in their schools. Individual teachers and teams of teachers have undertaken research across all curriculum areas in both primary and secondary schools. The following three examples give some indication of the diversity of interests of teachers working in Singapore schools.

A mathematics project was undertaken at McPherson Primary School. The purpose of this project was to explore, to test, and to develop confidence in mathematics ability and skills involving maths such as posing and solving problems. As a result of this project:

- Students are less anxious about learning Math. They are motivated;
- Students experience a sense of personal achievement in Math;
- Students are cognitively active while they learn;
- Students develop the ability to think clearly;
- Students are able to employ a variety of strategies to become mathematically literate;
- Teachers, who are committed to implementing strategies offered, maximise pupil learning. They are able to individualise instruction more precisely. This helps teachers determine clearly what students do or do not understand.

(Suan 1999)

A second project involved developing in teachers strategies to assist students in systematic risk-taking. As a result of this project participants would be able to use the strategy to help pupils not only to identify the reasons for their fear of taking risks but also to work out a plan to enable them to take risks.

Reflections on the project described by Eng Jee Nee from the Gifted Education Branch indicate that the strategy is time intensive, indeed that those involved in such a strategy should be prepared to follow students regularly and in some cases for as long as two years. Furthermore, the strategy itself involves a significant amount of self-disclosure, which could be disconcerting for some pupils. Trust is at the core of this process and all information should be kept confidential. For many students, engaging in such a project could be difficult, but through guidance and nurturing students lacking confidence could learn to become risk-takers (Nee 1999).

The third example is a project carried out by a history teacher, at St Theresa's Convent. This project involved examining the language use of teachers, the quality of talk and interaction that takes place when a teacher adopts an interpretive approach in the history classroom. It also examines the quality of talk of pupils when the history teacher gives them divergent thinking tasks. The teacher using an interpretive approach aims to give pupils the opportunity to use the history skills acquired by using project work. Here the emphasis is on learning by students rather than on the teacher teaching. The role of the teacher was to provide assistance and to allow students to question, while at the same time providing them with study frameworks to access and interpret information.

Not surprisingly, the nature and quality of the talk of the teacher and students was found to be important. As one teacher reflected, 'It is through talk that the past is interpreted. Teachers need to use language to give meaning and shape to difficult concepts' (Thuraisingam 1999).

One of the singular strengths of TN and its strategy in schools is celebration of good and innovative practice. TN hosts various opportunities and events for teachers to share the results of their research. Here teachers can give formal papers about their research or develop a poster exhibition and have their colleagues engage in a professional dialogue with them about their research. Research is published and disseminated to TN members. The pride, excitement and nervousness of teachers when they present their work to their peers are indicative of the personal and professional investment involved in participation. Its effect on others is generative and motivating and acts as a catalyst for other teachers to engage in such professional development.

The demand for support from TN to work with teachers in schools is currently greater than can be supplied by available resources. Clearly, here is a case where success is generating significant interest, and many want to be involved in the work of TN.

Learning from practice

The examples of transformative professionalism in practice presented here demonstrate the variety of systems and school-based initiatives that help to foster and build a new teacher professionalism. They provide evidence of what is possible at the system and individual levels and how it is possible to take leadership in change initiatives in order to meet local needs rather than externally imposed ones. There are many lessons that can be abstracted from the work and experiences of these four projects. I identify below seven which have practical and political currency in the broad project of establishing transformative teacher professionalism.

These projects all speak of the need for courage and conviction in building and sustaining new modes of professional engagement. They also emphasize the importance of local issues and interests in mobilizing teachers to engage in what, for some, would be a highly risky activity: researching your own practice and making the findings public. Finally, they also stress the importance of 'interruptions' to conventional wisdom about the nature of teachers' work and the nature of school reform.

Lessons learnt from the four projects

1   Local projects have greater currency

In each of these projects teachers working at local, regional and national levels have been given the opportunity to critically examine their own work practices in ways that would have been unlikely to happen when the immediate concerns of employing authorities or unions are themselves the concerns of teachers. These projects in different ways provide opportunities to open up spaces for the critical examination of classroom practice by teachers and others. In each project this remains a virtue that can live well beyond the life of the specific projects that have developed within the more general educational restructuring movement.

2   Developing research capabilities

Each of these projects has developed research capabilities in teachers and sees teacher or practitioner research as an important strategy for professional development. Ladwig *et al.* (1995: 22) maintain that 'building a research-based culture among teachers is a valuable way of building the systemic and organizational learning necessary to enable the change process in schools to be on-going, as continual re-interpretation of both the internal and external educational environment occurs'. It provides opportunities for teachers to look beyond some of their taken-for-granted assumptions about their own and their colleagues' practice. Teachers also acquire a range of data collection and interpretive skills which can help in the collective endeavour to improve student learning outcomes.

3   Collaborative action

Collaborative action is rooted in the processes and procedures of democratic participation. It breaks down teacher isolation and questions the conventional wisdom of individualism and privacy that characterizes many schools and classrooms. Ladwig *et al.* (1995) see collaborative action as a form of experience-based stewardship. Collaborative action acts as a strategy to interrupt and 'take stock' of what is happening in schools and classrooms. In every school, whether it was in Australia, Singapore or the USA, teachers were given ownership of school-specific issues rather than having to respond to externally imposed ones. These projects invited teachers, academics and others to create a common understanding of collaborative action through an acceptance of the responsibility that comes with bearing the knowledge of one's history (Ladwig *et al.* 1995).

Working collaboratively in teams also helped to maintain interest and high levels of energy among team members. Teachers were able to motivate and inspire each other, test ideas, debate strategies and negotiate shared meanings about their practice and the projects that were being undertaken in their schools.

4   *Professional and cultural readiness*

For teachers to engage in this type of reform work where their own work comes under a critical gaze not only requires a high level or trust and risk-taking but also implies a professional and cultural readiness to undertake such work. Ladwig *et al.* (1995: 44) claim that:

> Changing the cultural base must accompany changing the structure of work organization; changing the cultural base means gaining the support of a critical mass of staff in a school; and changing teachers' perspectives often takes longer than changing their work practices.

While reculturing and restructuring are two complementary processes in any school reform initiative, one has to precede the other to ensure a successful reform outcome. As Ladwig *et al.* (1995) found out in their work with the NSN, schools that embarked on restructuring before reculturing often met professional resistance. Establishing a shared philosophical base and getting teachers' thinking right was axiomatic and often took longer than anticipated. Flexibility in terms of timelines and expectations goes hand in hand with professional and cultural readiness.

5   *Leadership*

In each of these examples, leadership was important. It did not need to be that exercised by the most senior person in the school, even though that was important. It was the intellectual leadership and often courage demonstrated by individuals or groups that provided the motivation for other staff members to take risks and to open up their classrooms for outside scrutiny. Certainly the support of the schools' senior executive gave the project a legitimacy and status in the eyes of people within and outside of the school. Conversely, if the project was not given priority in the school by the senior executive its life expectancy was often short.

Importantly, when leadership was devolved to teachers they had to have the authority to act, or, as Currie *et al.* (1996: 70) state:

> authority to implement a clear intellectual vision for the learning of all students is a central requirement for school organizational capacity. When school action is constrained by external regulation it is difficult for staff to feel a sense of ownership or collective responsibility for the school's success. Schools most able to build a professional community experienced high levels of autonomy to act and teacher influence over their work in the school.

In short, the conditions that helped to facilitate successful projects and school change revolved around the structural conditions in the school and the quality of leadership practised by various staff within the school.

6 *External support*

In each of these projects the work that was undertaken was facilitated by the allocation of external funding support. Schools need financial, technical and political support to undertake major reform projects. Currie *et al.* (1996: 70) argue that:

> External stakeholders can help schools focus on student learning and enhance organizational capacity by setting standards for learning of high intellectual quality, providing sustained staff development and implementing deregulation to increase school autonomy. Sometimes external sources can undermine school organizational capacity by pulling schools in different directions, imposing unreasonable regulations and by instigating rapid shifts in policy and leadership.

These projects at one stage or another required various forms of advocacy either from within the school or external to it in order to gain legitimacy in the eyes of community groups, parents or educational bureaucracies. The ability to mobilize or garner interest from influential people cannot be underestimated. This external take on the importance of the project or its outcomes often helps to sustain and embed those outcomes into the ongoing practices and structures of the school.

7 *Knowledge generation*

Each of the projects described here was concerned with putting into use professional and practical knowledge generated by students and teachers. While different processes and strategies were put in place to achieve this, the types of knowledge generated made important contributions to the developing knowledge base of classroom practice and student learning. Furthermore, each of these projects demonstrated that people take seriously the realities of curriculum development, teaching, assessment and the lives of students and teachers who must cooperate to make schools work (Apple and Beane 1999).

Knowledge generation and learning go hand in hand in establishing a transformative professionalism. Learning transforms who we are and what we do, and consequently involves the development of new teacher identities. The issue of new or emerging teacher professional identities is taken up in the next chapter.

Conclusion

Each of the projects described here provides examples of what is possible when teachers work collaboratively on joint enterprises which aim at improving student learning outcomes and the working relationships and conditions of teachers. They have all required strong commitment in terms of time and energy and high levels of trust and risk-taking. Nevertheless, they provide a variety of approaches to enhance teacher professionalism that emerge from the profession itself. This kind of grassroots work is the future for a different kind of teacher professionalism. It provides the basis for the development of an activist teaching profession.

Notes

1 More information about the NSN can be found on its website www.nsn.net.au
2 This is the name of the local indigenous group.
3 More information about CES can be found on its website www.essentialschools. org/aboutus/phil/chapter/ceschapter.html

seven

New professional identities for new times

Issues of teacher professionalism and teacher professional identity are now evident in much research literature emerging from the USA, UK and Australia. Recent education reforms and the associated changes in working conditions and professional expectations have meant that issues of teacher professionalism and professional identity are being contested at both the level of policy and practice. Indeed, as presented in Chapter 1, current debates in the public and scholarly arena indicate that there are competing views about the nature of teacher professionalism. Furthermore, in some instances debates still circulate about whether or not teaching is a profession. What counts as teacher professionalism has come to be a site of struggle between various interest groups concerned with the broader enterprise of education. Some would say that it is in the best interests of government that teaching should not be seen as a profession as it gives greater opportunity for regulative control of the profession. Others would suggest that, given the specialised knowledge base of teachers, the increased demand for professional standards and the greater demand for teachers to see themselves as knowledge workers, then teachers have earned the status of being a profession in a more orthodox sense (Brint 1994).

In Chapter 2 I identified the dominant discourses that are shaping teacher professionalism in Australia and elsewhere. These discourses, which are best described as a set of related social practices, are composed of:

> ways of talking, listening, reading, writing acting, interacting, believing, valuing and using tools and objects in particular settings and at specific times, so as to display or to recognise a particular social identity. . . . The Discourse creates social positions (or perspectives) from which people

are 'invited' ('summoned') to speak, listen, act, read and write, think, feel, believe and value in certain characteristic, historically recognisable ways, in combination with their own individual style and creativity. . . . Discourses create, produce, and reproduce opportunities for people to be and recognise certain *kinds of people*.

(Gee *et al.* 1996: 10, italics in original)

Ball (1994) argues that the discourse of management is a key feature of current reform initiatives. He maintains that 'in a variety of ways it articulates a new culture of schooling, a culture of commodification and output indicators which articulates with the culture of choice and relative advantage to which parents are being drawn' (Ball 1994: 65–6). Management here, according to Ball (1994: 66–7), 'is both a body of precepts, assumptions and theory, to be learned by managers, and a set of practices to be implemented, encompassing both managers and managed'.

Three variations within educational discourses relating to educational policy in general and self-management in schools in particular shape current educational debates: financial management, entrepreneurial management and professional management. Each of these has different effects in terms of the work of management and the outcomes of particular initiatives that emerge from these. Financial management begins with a concern with balancing the books, with maximizing the budget and doing educationally what can be afforded (Ball 1994: 68). A close relationship exists between financial management discourse and entrepreneurial management. Here responsiveness, competition, diversification and income generation are prominent in the manager's lexicon (Ball 1994). Finally, professional discourse is articulated around a development and planning perspective.

Earlier, I argued that discourses circulating around democratic and managerial professionalism were shaping current educational debates, policies and practices. I suggest that democratic professionalism is emerging from the profession itself and that managerialist professionalism is being reinforced by employing authorities through their policies on teacher professional development with their emphasis on accountability and effectiveness. The purpose of these is to shape the way teachers think, talk and act in relation to themselves as teachers individually and collectively. In this chapter I examine the types of professional identity emerging from dominant discourses and the influence that these have on the collective teaching profession in order to provide moral and intellectual leadership for it.

Depending upon the contexts in which teachers are working and how they negotiate and make meaning of these, discourses will construct particular identities for teachers in their professional lives. I identify two forms of teacher professional identity that are emerging in response to current educational and public sector reforms. I argue that entrepreneurial teacher professional identity is emerging out of managerial discourses and that activist identities are developing in response to the democratic discourses.[1] Importantly, these identities are not fixed, and in many cases teachers would be unlikely to locate themselves in one or other of these categories. Rather, depending on the context, teachers would move from one to the other in response to particular exigencies as they develop.

Recent reforms, particularly those concerning devolution and marketization, have encouraged the development of a set of paradoxes about the nature of teaching as a profession and about the professional identity and professional development of teachers. The first paradox is that the call for teacher professionalism related to a revisioning of occupational identity is occurring at a time when there is evidence that teachers are being deskilled and their work intensified. The second is that, while it is acknowledged that rethinking classroom practice is exceptionally demanding, fewer resources are being allocated to teacher learning. Third, the teaching profession is being exhorted to be autonomous while at the same time it is under increasing surveillance by politicians and the community to be more accountable through standards regimes and rituals of verification (Power 1997). As a consequence of the paradoxes underpinning the changes in education policy and practice, the very idea of teacher professionalism and professional identity is in a state of flux.

Identity is the way that people understand their own individual experience and how they act and identify with various groups. Castells (1997: 6) indicates the complexity of identity and the relationship between individuals, institutions and organizations in its construction:

> By identity, as it refers to social actors, I understand the process of construction of meaning on the basis of cultural attribute, or related set of cultural attributes, that is/are given priority over other sources of meaning. For a given individual, or for a collective actor, there may be a plurality of identities. Yet, such a plurality is a source of stress and contradiction in both self representation and social action. This is because identity must be distinguished from what traditionally, sociologists have called roles, and role sets. Roles (for example, to be a worker, a mother, a neighbour, a socialist militant, a union member, a basketball player, a church goer, and a smoker, at the same time) are defined by norms structured by the institutions and organisations of society. Their relative weight in influencing people's behaviour depends upon negotiations and arrangements between individuals and these institutions and organisations. Identities are sources of meaning for the actors themselves, and by themselves, constructed through the process of individuation.

The construction of identities uses building materials from history, from geography, from biology, from productive and reproductive institutions, from collective memory and from personal fantasies, from power apparatuses and religious revelations (Castells 1997: 7). As Castells goes on to argue, 'individuals, social groups, and societies process all these materials, and rearrange their meaning, according to social determinations and cultural projects that are rooted in their social structure and their in space/time framework'.

Professional identity

In terms of its orthodox uses, the idea of professional identity is rarely seen as problematical. It is used to refer to a set of externally ascribed attributes that differentiate one group from another. Professional identity is thus a set of attributes that are imposed upon the teaching profession either by outsiders or by members of the teaching fraternity itself. It provides a shared set of attributes, values and so on that enable teachers as a group to be differentiated from other groups. From this perspective it is an exclusive rather than inclusive ideal and is conservative rather than radical in its intent. Following Epstein, identity is in essence a concept of synthesis, integration and action: 'It represents the process by which the person seeks to integrate his [sic] various statuses and roles, as well as his diverse experiences, into a coherent image of self' (Epstein 1978: 101).

Under current conditions of change, uncertainty and continuous educational restructuring, managerialist or democratic teacher professional identities emerge out of what Bernstein (1996) refers to as retrospective and prospective identities. The retrospective identities use as resources narratives of the past that provide exemplars and criteria for the present and the future. A subset of the retrospective identity, the elitist identity, uses a narrative of the past to provide exemplars, criteria and standards of conduct. It is an amalgam of knowledge, sensitivities and manners, of education and upbringing (Bernstein 1996: 78). Alternatively, prospective identities are in essence future-oriented. They may well use and rest upon narrative resources, but the narrative resources of prospective identity constructions ground the identity in the future. As Bernstein (1996: 79) argues, 'prospective identities change the basis for collective recognition and relation'. Prospective identities are launched by social movements, and are engaged in conversion through their engagement with economic and political activity to provide for the development of their new potential. For Castells (1997), project identity is a form of identity-building. Project identity occurs when social actors, on the basis of whichever cultural materials are available to them, build a new identity that redefines their position in society, and by so doing seek the transformation of the overall social structure (Castells 1997: 8). The concepts of prospective identities and project identity provide a useful starting point for rethinking teacher professional identity. While both refer more to broad-based social movements that have the transformation of the overall social structure as their outcome, they point to the possibility of the emergence of a new identity. Furthermore, they support a form of collective action by teachers that is industrial, political and professional. The industrial component comes through the activities of teacher unions focusing on work conditions, remuneration and social recognition, as well as on issues of teacher professional development activities. The Teaching Accord between unions and government in Australia in the early 1990s marked out possibilities for this to happen (see Seddon 1996; Sachs 1997).[2] Finally, it is political, for, as Kathleen Casey (1993: 158) argues, 'although the political is everywhere, it is not diffuse, for everyone is involved but not in the same way'.

In times of rapid change, identity cannot be seen to be a fixed thing; it is negotiated, open, shifting, ambiguous, the result of culturally available meanings and the open-ended power-laden enactment of those meanings in everyday situations (Kondo 1990: 24). For teachers this is mediated by their own experience in schools and outside of schools as well as their own beliefs and values about what it means to be a teacher and the type of teacher they aspire to be.

Wenger (1998: 149) distinguishes five dimensions of identity:

(i)   identity *as negotiated experiences* where we define who we are by the ways we experience our selves through participation as well as the way we and others reify our selves;

(ii)   identity *as community membership* where we define who we are by the familiar and the unfamiliar;

(iii)   identity *as learning trajectory* where we define who we are by where we have been and where are going;

(iv)   identity *as nexus of multi membership* where we define who we are by the ways we reconcile our various forms of identity into one identity; and

(v)   identity *as a relation between the local and the global* where we define who we are by negotiating local ways of belonging to broader constellations and manifesting broader styles and discourses.

Identity here is about how teachers define themselves through their experience and the factors that mediate that experience and how meaning is attributed to these experiences. A reconceptualized notion of teacher professional identity needs to incorporate these five dimensions of identity as they address the social, cultural and political (macro and micro, individual and group) aspects of identity formation. Such a multidimensional view of professional identity helps us to understand the complexity of teachers' work and how they come to understand their work and their sense of themselves as teachers.

Importantly, identity and practice mirror each other. As Wenger (1998: 149) argues, 'there is a profound connection between identity and practice. Developing a practice requires the formation of a community whose members can engage with one another and thus acknowledge each other as participants'. For teachers, the conditions in which they work, in particular the organization and structure of the schools where they work and the narratives they construct to represent their experiences, facilitate a strong orientation towards practice in its various forms.

Clearly then, within the context of uncertainty and multiple educational restructurings, teachers' professional identity is not straightforward. There would be incongruities between the defined identity of teachers as proposed by systems, unions and individual teachers themselves, and these will change according to contextual and individual factors and exigencies. Identity must for ever be re-established and negotiated. It defines our capacity to speak and act autonomously and allows for the differentiation of ourselves from others while continuing to be the same person (Melucci 1996). For teachers, this is a challenge given that governments do not see it to be in their best interests to have a vocal and autonomous teaching service. When teachers do act autonomously their behaviour is often not sanctioned by their employing authorities, but rather chastised. Nevertheless the creation of a strong professional identity is what distinguishes the expertise of teachers which differentiates them from other workers.

It may not be productive to talk about professional identity in an essentialised way. Clearly teachers inhabit multiple professional identities. For a primary school teacher, for example, these might include the general category of primary teacher. However, this identity can be broken down into further identities by year level or subject/discipline. These people not only may see themselves as belonging to the generic category of primary teacher but may also identify with their area of specialization and year level. A similar logic follows in secondary schools but with more categories for differentiation along subject/discipline, year level lines. For Castells (1997: 7), the distinction between role and identity is simple: identities organize the meaning whereas roles organize the function. This is important in terms of teacher professional identity, for teachers working inside schools assume a variety of roles in their schools and classroom – primary teacher, grade 4 teacher, netball coach – and outside of the school they may be parents, community activists, gardeners and so on. For our purposes here, it is the meaning attributed to being a teacher that is important.

While any idea of a fixed teacher professional identity is unproductive, nevertheless it can serve the needs of the state by providing a framework for externally initiated controls. These controls set the limits for what can be said about teacher professional identity and at the same time define what must remain unsaid on pain of censure. In such situations, teacher professional identity serves bureaucratic purposes in so far as control of debates about its meaning is taken away from the people who 'live' it on a daily basis, the teachers themselves. Importantly, as Kathleen Casey's life history work on teachers reinforces, it is the collective stories rather than the individual stories that provide the political impetus for ongoing action. These stories provide examples of professionalism in action and professionalism for action. They also give a clear sense of the individual and collective power of identity.

The entrepreneurial identity

Recent educational reforms in Australia, the UK and New Zealand have been based on the logic of the new public sector reform agenda. These reforms have sought to make educational bureaucracies more accountable and to engage them in practices derived from the business world. Here, management serves two purposes in the reform process: means and end. In other words:

> management (as synonym for efficiency) is taken to be 'the one best way' to organize and run schools, and to the extent that management culture embraces enterprise and commercialism it shifts schools away from a 'culture of welfare' to a 'culture of profit and production' – that is management does profound ideological work in relation to the conception and conduct of schooling.
>
> (Ball 1994: 71)

Accordingly, new forms of control have been mandated in policy decisions and educational practices. One significant outcome of these initiatives is the credo of:

> 'doing more with less' in a context of a competitive educational market. Schools are expected to compete for additional resources and to meet the needs of 'consumers'. Corporate managerial control is the modus operandi. This form of control involves a complex mix of control through the invisible hand of the market, centralized prescriptive curriculum control, an ideology informed by such values as enterprise, competition and choice . . .
>
> (Smyth *et al.* 2000: 43)

A new teacher professional with an aligned identity is thus emerging: what Menter *et al.* (1997) refer to as the 'entreprencurial professional' who will identify with the efficient, responsible and accountable version of service that is currently being promulgated by the state. Du Gay (1996: 181) observes that 'because previously distinct forms of life or modes of conduct are now classified primarily, if not exclusively, as "enterprise forms" the conceptions and practices of personhood they give rise to are remarkably consistent'. Thus, there is the emergence of what Catherine Casey (1995) refers to as 'designer employees' who are responding to a broad crisis in industrial production, work organization and culture. Education bureaucracies too would encourage 'designer teachers' who consistently demonstrate compliance to policy imperatives and perform at high levels of efficiency and effectiveness. They must also demonstrate consistent high quality teaching, measured by externally set performance indicators. The logic is that these teachers must be compliant employees who accept standards regimes while at the same time ensuring that the learning outcomes of all students are improved.

Fergusson (1994: 106–7) has the following to say regarding the consequences of managerialism for the teaching profession:

> The potential impact on the constitution, standing, identity, autonomy and authority of the profession is enormous. The socialization of intending teachers into the mores, values, understandings of what it means to be a teacher will switch from being developed in a collective setting of debate informed by theory, research and evidence, to one in which socialization is entirely dependent on two or three teachers. New teachers' capacities to act autonomously, work independently and most of all mount well-grounded challenges to managerial diktat are likely to diminish, and their sense of membership and solidarity of a larger body to be diluted.

Menter *et al.* (1997: 57) maintain that 'judgement about priorities, appropriateness and efficacy, once the preserve of the expert, guided by rules and precedent, is ignored or excluded'. The version of teacher professionalism which is imbued in public sector reform agendas has profound consequences for both teachers' work and teacher professional identity.

Under managerialist discourses the market will play an important part in how teachers constitute their professional identity collectively and individually. Competition between schools for reduced resources gives rise to a competitive ethos rather than a collaborative one. The efficient operation of the market is fostered through the combination of legislative controls and internal, institutional mechanisms, notably performance indicators and inspections, which ostensibly provide consumers with a basis for selection but more importantly provide managerial imperatives (Menter *et al.* 1997: 64). Under such conditions, the rise of the teacher professional standards movement in the UK, USA and Australia can be seen to be concerned more with standardization of practice than with quality, despite a public rhetoric for the latter. The issue of professional standards was discussed earlier; suffice it to say that the instigation of a standards regime is not politically neutral nor is its agenda in the best interests of an autonomous teaching profession.

New Zealand is a case in point where managerialism and marketization have characterized education policy and practice from the late 1980s. Standardized measures of performance enable schools to be ranked by their customers, market competition penalizes non-conformity in teaching and learning, and the national curriculum functions as a system of cultural control, 'a standardised language, a narrative history of national destiny, so a normative, monocultural definition of community claiming the legitimacy of familiar values and an external identity' (Marginson 1997: 190). Putting education into the marketplace means making education appear more like a commodity so that parents are given access to a range of products from which they can select. In this framework, schools become more efficient in response to competition (Menter *et al.* 1997: 26).

In the UK, the intention of the New Right policies in education are aimed at removing costs and responsibilities from the state in order to improve efficiency and responsiveness as a means of raising standards of performance. What the state fails to acknowledge is the agency of teachers collectively and individually in such an enterprise. There is an assumption about the nature of teachers and how they will receive and interpret the standards. Indeed, there is a preferred reading of standards. Mahony and Hextall (2000: 79) make the telling point that:

> In order to 'meet the Standards' you have to be the kind of person that the standards have in mind, capable of accomplishing the activities that the Standards entail, living with and conducting the relationships presumed at different levels, and of working within the assumptions which form the Standards boundaries.

As recent work in the UK by Mahony and Hextall (2000) and Furlong *et al.* (2000) has demonstrated, the generation, form and content of the standards has generated significant debate among the teaching profession. Furthermore, as Mahony and Hextall's research has indicated, in terms of 'fitness for purpose' the standards are seen as providing helpful guidelines for setting agendas for professional development sensitive to the local context. However, these standards do not resolve issues of consistency and fairness when used for assessment purposes, and rely heavily on interpretation for translation into practice.

Under managerialist conditions, a cult of individualism has the possibility to reinfect the occupational culture of teachers. This individualism develops in response to teachers' working conditions and is characterized by isolation and privacy. As Andy Hargreaves (1992: 171) observes, 'individualism is primarily a shortcoming, not a strength, not a possibility; something to be removed rather than something to be respected'. In many cases the history, structure and architecture of schools help to reinforce such an individualistic culture. Such cultures certainly work towards the maintenance of conservative, even reactionary, practice and stand in opposition to a generative or change-embracing culture. Individualism is in stark contrast to collaboration and collegiality that are the cornerstones of democratic discourses and the development of an activist professional identity. The entrepreneurial identity, then, is:

- individualistic
- competitive
- controlling and regulative
- externally defined
- standards-led.

The activist identity

Much of the basis of democratic schooling is premised on the framework developed by John Dewey (1916) in *Democracy and Education*. It is worth noting Dewey's position:

> In order to have large numbers of values in common, all the members of the group must have an equitable opportunity to receive and take from others. There must be a large variety of shared undertakings and experiences. Otherwise, the influences which educate some into masters educate others into slaves. And the experiences of each party loses in meaning when the free interchange of varying modes of life experiences is arrested.
>
> (1916: 84)

Schools in which democratic discourses inform all aspects of school life do not happen by chance, they require strategy and commitment. They result from explicit attempts by educators to put in place arrangements and opportunities that will bring democracy to life (Apple and Beane 1999). They require the two forms of activity: putting into place democratic structures and processes, and creating a curriculum that will give students democratic experiences (Apple and Beane 1999). It is the former that is the focus of attention here. The focus is on participation and inclusion of all involved in the educational enterprise. The complexity of this is captured by Apple and Beane (1999: 10), who suggest that:

> all of those directly involved in the school, including young children, have the right to participate in the process of decision making. For this reason, democratic schools are marked by widespread participation in

issues of governance and policy making. Committees, councils and other school wide decision-making groups include not only professional educators, but also young people, their parents and other members of the school community.

An activist identity emerging from democratic discourses has clear emancipatory aims. The conditions under which an activist identity has opportunities to emerge and flourish are described by Beane and Apple (1995: 6–7) as:

- The open flow of ideas, regardless of their popularity, that enables people to be as fully informed as possible.
- Faith in the individual and collective capacity of people to create possibilities for resolving problems.
- The use of critical reflection and analysis to evaluate ideas, problems and policies.
- Concern for the welfare of others and 'the common good'.
- Concern for the dignity and rights of individuals and minorities.
- An understanding that democracy is not so much an 'ideal' to be pursued as an 'idealized' set of values that we must live and that must guide our life as people.
- The organization of social institutions to promote and extend the democratic way of life.

First and foremost an activist identity found in democratic schools is concerned to reduce or eliminate exploitation, inequality and oppression. Accordingly, the development of this identity is deeply rooted in principles of equity and social justice. These are not only for the teaching profession but also for a broader education constituency of parents and students.

Deliberative democracy is a foundation upon which an activist identity is located. Gutmann and Thompson suggest that deliberation should extend throughout the political process. Its forums embrace virtually any setting in which citizens come together on a regular basis to reach collective decisions about public issues. 'Deliberative democracy asks citizens and officials to justify public policy by giving reasons that can be accepted by those bound by it. This disposition to seek mutually justifiable reasons expresses the core of the process of deliberation' (Gutmann and Thompson 1996: 34). Furthermore, this is central to democratic discourses and the sustaining of an activist identity.

Earlier I suggested that a revised professional identity requires a new form of professionalism and engagement. Redefining teacher professional identity as an activist identity involves two main elements. The first is a sustained effort to shed the shackles of the past, thereby permitting a transformative attitude towards the future. The second is overcoming the legitimate or the illegitimate domination of some individuals or groups.

In order to achieve this redefinition I suggest two interconnected strategies. First, the teaching profession at the individual and collective level should acknowledge the importance of professional self-narratives (Gergen and Gergen 1988). These are culturally provided stories about selves and their passage through lives that provide resources drawn upon by individuals in their interactions with one another and with themselves. Stories provide a compelling basis for change or for affirmations. For Gergen and Gergen (1988: 20–1):

> narratives are, in effect, social constructions, undergoing continuous alteration as interaction progresses . . . the self-narrative is a linguistic implement constructed by people in relationships to sustain, enhance or impede various actions. Self-narratives are symbolic systems used for such social purposes as justification, criticism and social solidification.

The teachers themselves construct these self-narratives, as they relate to their social, political and professional agendas. These self-narratives are stories of stories; they are reflexive in that they are understood both by the individual whose stories they are and by others who may have similar experiences. For teachers, these self-narratives are often tacit, they operate at the level of the taken-for-granted. They are developed during their own schooling and teacher education and are then embedded and reinforced in the course of their professional lives in schools and so on.

These self-narratives provide both a glue for a collective professional identity and a provocation for renewing teacher professionalism. It is important that stories are made public, not necessarily in a written sense but at least communicated in a way that means they can be shared, debated and contested by others. I suggest that making these narratives public is a source for lively professional development. It provides opportunities for teachers to communicate with each other about what they think schooling, education, subject knowledge, pedagogy and so on are about. Furthermore, it acts as a provocation to institute a more active, spirited debate about policy and practice. Critical self-narratives about professional identity at the individual and collective levels have clear emancipatory objectives. These objectives, I suggest, are towards an activist stance and the development of an activist identity. In what follows I identify a protocol for an activist professional and describe the conditions that would help facilitate its development.

Those involved in democratic schools see themselves as participants of communities of learning, or what Wenger (1998) refers to as communities of practice. By their very nature these communities are diverse, and that diversity is highly prized, not viewed as a problem (Apple and Beane 1999). These communities of learning or practice are not self-contained entities; they develop in larger contexts – historical, social, cultural, institutional – with specific reference to resources and constraints. Some of these conditions and requirements are explicitly articulated. Some are implicit but no less binding (Wenger 1998: 79). Within these communities there are various levels of expertise that should be seen as a shared set of professional resources. They require sustained engagement, and at the same time demand the development and negotiation of shared meanings. They are not intrinsically beneficial or harmful. Nor are they privileged in terms of positive or negative effects. Nevertheless, they are a force to be reckoned with. Wenger (1998: 85) argues, 'as a locus of engagement in action, interpersonal relations, shared knowledge, and negotiation of enterprises, such communities hold the key to real transformation – the kind that has real effects on people's lives'. Communities of practice that articulate around issues of professional practice can have profound impacts on teachers' lives both in terms of their classroom practice and in terms of how they construct their professional identities which are exercised both inside and outside of schools.

For Wenger (1998), there are two core dimensions in the operation of these communities of practice, namely the work of engagement and the work of imagination. The work of engagement requires the ability to take part in meaningful activities and interactions, in the production of sharable artefacts, in community-building conversations, and in the negotiation of new situations (Wenger 1998: 184). The work of imagination requires the ability to disengage. Wenger (1998: 185) suggests that imagination needs:

> the willingness, freedom, energy and time to expose ourselves to the exotic, move around, try new identities, and explore new relations. It requires the ability to proceed without being too quick within the constraints of a specific form of accountability, to accept non-participation as an adventure, and to suspend judgment.

The work of engagement and imagination is fundamental to the development of an activist professional identity. Both provide the structural and affective conditions for the role of teacher activist to be legitimated, recognized and practised.

Communities of practice, then, provide the context and conditions for teachers to be strategic and tactical in order to develop an activist identity. They facilitate values of respect, reciprocity and collaboration. Communities of practice and an activist identity are coextensive, each nourishes and supports the other. These values cannot exist in isolation or without a purpose. The purpose is to revitalize teachers' sense of themselves professionally and personally. Importantly, this is an individual and collective activity, provoked from inside as well as from outside the profession.

The search for a new identity could be interpreted as an attempt to change the public perception of the role and purpose of teachers and teaching. Teachers, bureaucrats, unions, academics and others are attempting to adopt new professional identities at a stage when public policies and debates about schooling and teacher professionalism are under close scrutiny. The challenge for those involved in the broader political project of revitalizing issues of teacher professionalism and professional identity is how to facilitate public debate about the nature of teaching. This means addressing various issues which might include dealing with the challenges of working under conditions of rapid change, ambiguity and uncertainty, while at the same time having a clear and articulated sense of what it means to be a teacher in contemporary society.

This challenge needs to be taken up by teacher educators, teacher unions, employing bodies and the community in general. Clearly, an activist identity is not straightforward, nor is it something that is easily acquired in a climate where managerialism is strong. Nevertheless, it is an aspiration that works strongly in the interests of students and the communities in which schools are located.

In summary, then, an activist identity is:

- based on democratic principles
- negotiated
- collaborative
- socially critical
- future-oriented
- strategic and tactical.

Conclusion

In this chapter I have argued that two discourses have dominated education debate, policy and practice in recent times. I have suggested that these discourses and the assumptions that inform them provoke two quite distinct forms of teacher professional identity. The managerialist discourse fosters an entrepreneurial identity in which the market and issues of accountability, economy, efficiency and effectiveness shape how teachers individually and collectively construct their professional identities. Alternatively, democratic discourses, which are in distinct contrast to the managerialist ones, support an activist professional identity in which collaborative cultures are an integral part of teachers' work practices. These democratic discourses provide the conditions for the development of communities of learning or practice. They are concerned not only with engaging with some enterprise but also with understanding how this engagement fits in the broader scheme of things (Wenger 1998). These communities of practice are collegial, negotiated and they form and reform around specific issues. Notwithstanding this, there is a need to defend some of the older identities.

Sometimes the call for the 'new' can act in ways that support managerialism, as it sees itself as 'new'. Hence the creation of professional identities builds on, rather than rejects, previous notions. Accordingly, it requires a form of reflexivity when what has come previously is used a resource to build upon.

New times and conditions require alternative forms of teacher professionalism and teacher identities to develop. Furlong *et al.* (2000: 175) suggest that:

> we need to ask some fundamental questions about who does have a legitimate right to be involved in defining teaching professionalism. Are state control and market forces or professional self governance really the only models of accountability available to us – or can we develop new approaches to teacher professionalism, based upon more participatory relationships with diverse communities?

The search for a new identity sometimes assumes that such an identity already exists and wants to be discovered. This may be correct only if the new identity is to be written by someone else (Czarniawska 1997). If the teaching profession wants to be the author of its own identity or professional narrative then now is possibly the time for this to occur. There is now some evidence suggesting that the market is no longer the appropriate metaphor or structure in which education policies and practices develop. Under more democratic conditions, where teacher knowledge and expertise are recognized and rewarded, an activist teacher professional identity fosters new forms of public and professional engagement by teachers themselves and the broader population. Activist teacher professional identity encourages new forms of association of teachers among themselves and with others. It promotes new work practices and more flexible ways of thinking about practice.

Teachers' professional identities are rich and complex because they are produced in a rich and complex set of relations of practice (Wenger 1998: 162). This richness and complexity needs to be nurtured and developed in conditions where there is respect, mutuality and communication. An activist teacher professional identity is not something that will come naturally to all teachers. It has to be negotiated, lived and practised. The development of such an identity will be a challenge for many, and will be challenged by others, but once its elements are learnt and communicated across the teaching fraternity it will make a significant contribution to teachers' work and how they experience and make sense of that work. Teacher identity stands at the core of the teaching profession. It provides a framework for teachers to construct their own ideas of 'how to be', 'how to act' and 'how to understand' their work and their place in society. Importantly, teacher identity is something that is neither fixed nor imposed; it is negotiated through experience and the sense that is made of that experience.

Notes

1 I acknowledge that there are problems associated with using binary oppositions, in particular the simplification of complex ideas into convenient couplets. Nevertheless, for the purposes of this chapter these two identities and discourses at one level do appear to be oppositional. However, we should be cognizant of how managerial discourses are seeking to redefine and reconfigure democracy such that democracy is no longer a social project but rather an economic one (see Apple 1993).

2 In Australia the project of reclaiming teacher professionalism had its antecedents in industrial and professional activities during the late 1980s and early 1990s. Specifically, award restructuring at the federal level provided the impetus for school reform and the promise for teacher professionalism. The necessary ideological conditions within teaching and outside it were created to facilitate debate about the scope and nature of teacher professionalism. The Teaching Accord of 1993 constituted a tangible recognition of the fundamental role that teachers must play in the development of the profession. The Teaching Accord established priorities and detailed the commitment of the Commonwealth to the involvement of the profession and its financial support for professional development, curriculum assessment and research projects with seed funding for national teacher professional development projects.

eight

The activist teacher professional

In earlier chapters I have described and analysed the changing contexts, discourses and pressures on teacher professionalism in Australia and elsewhere. I made the distinction between old and transformative professionalism and indicated that the way forward in order to enhance the status of teaching and to improve the working conditions of teachers was through the general project and strategy exemplified by transformative teacher professionalism. In this chapter I elaborate the dimensions of transformative professionalism through what I refer to as the activist teacher professional. Here I draw together some of the issues that have been developed throughout the book and I formulate a conceptual framework for the development of an activist teacher professional. I also establish a protocol as the platform for mobilizing teachers and finally I present two strategies for how this might be operationalized.

In developing an argument for an activist teacher professionalism, I draw on the work of Anthony Giddens (1994) in *Beyond Left and Right: The Future of Radical Politics*, especially his concepts of active trust and generative politics. These concepts help in rethinking the macro and micro social and political dimensions of teacher professionalism and move it in a more activist direction. They extend David Hargreaves' (1994) idea of new professionalism, which he suggests 'involves movement away from the teacher's traditional authority and autonomy towards new forms of relationship with colleagues, with students, and with parents. These relationships are becoming closer as well as more intense and collaborative, involving more explicit negotiation of roles and responsibilities' (1994: 424). Furthermore, also like McLaughlin's (1997) new professionalism, activist professionalism moves the focus for analysis and action from the individual to the group.

Active trust needs to be embedded in the group and it is from that group that generative politics can spring.

This kind of teacher professionalism has strong roots in more orthodox definitions of professionalism – in terms of *expertise* (the possession by an occupational group of exclusive knowledge and practice), *altruism* (an ethical concern by this group for its clients) and *autonomy* (the professional's need and right to exercise control over entry into, and subsequent practice within, that particular occupation (Bottery 1996: 179–80). At the same time, though, it differs from orthodox or classical views in that its fundamental purpose is political. It brings together alliances and networks of various educational interest groups for collective action to improve *all* aspects of the education enterprise at the macro level and student learning outcomes and teachers' status in the eyes of the community at the micro level. It is premised on three fundamental questions: (1) What is the best place to accomplish the project of becoming activist professionals in teaching? (2) What is the best place for ME to be? (3) What can I do from where I am?

Activist teacher professionalism

The development of an activist teaching profession is premised on three concepts: trust, active trust and generative politics. The concepts provide the necessary conditions for a politics of transformation to emerge and be sustained. The interplay between these three concepts provides the conceptual platform for an activist teaching profession to be developed.

Trust

There appear to be conflicting views about public trust in contemporary society, especially trust in policy-makers. Fukuyama (1999), for example, argues that there is a decline in trust in public institutions, particularly older ones associated with authority and coercion such as the military, police, the church and so on. Earlier work by Lipset and Schneider (1987) concludes that public trust in policy-makers has declined over time in the USA and elsewhere. Cvetkovich and Lofstedt (1999: 6) suggest that 'distrust does seem to be related to views about the overall state of the nation, particularly people's perception of the moral climate . . . distrust is related to disillusion and frustration not anger. Furthermore, much of the disillusionment is directed at political leaders'. Alternatively, Etzioni (1996) in his book *The New Golden Rule*, argues that, since 1990, public trust in policy-makers and society as a whole is actually increasing (cited in Cvetkovic and Lofstedt 1999). Commentators, then, are undecided about whether trust is diminishing and distrust is increasing. Nevertheless, trust is at the core of the continued functioning and effectiveness of a democratic society. For our purposes here, there is evidence to suggest that trust of the teaching profession by the state is decreasing. This evidence consists in the imposition of regimes of accountability, policies to measure teacher competence through standard-setting, school inspections and so on.

The question that must be asked first is, what is trust in general and social trust in particular? Trust operates at both an interpersonal (micro) and a system (macro) level. Macro-level and micro-level trust play a mutually reinforcing role. Bradbury *et al.* (1999: 120) suggest that 'system level trust appears to establish the context in which social relationships occur, while the establishment of trust on the micro level may also contribute to confidence at the social level'.

Trust has a variety of functions in society. First, trust is important in reducing complexity. It acts as a form of social shorthand. If it is not there you have to ensure that every structure is consistent in the messages that individuals or groups are trying to impart. It is critical to the predictability and reliability of interactions, as, for example, through roles and routines (Misztal 1996). Earle and Cvetkovich (1999) argue that social trust is based on shared cultural values developed in tandem with complexity in society. They suggest that social trust is a simplifying strategy that enables individuals to adapt to complex social environments and thereby benefit from increased social opportunities.

Second, trust contributes to cohesion – the formation of the basis of self-identity and, hence, relationships to the wider world. This is how trust relates to the area of collaboration – to the fostering of mutual respect and solidarity among persons with different perspectives, a form of social capital that benefits the larger community (cited in Bradbury *et al.* 1999).

Trust involves an element of risk and uncertainty. Misztal (1996) emphasizes that to trust 'is more than believing'; it involves 'expectations about something future or contingent on a future occasion' (cited in Bradbury *et al.* 1999: 121). From this perspective, trust is based on the assumption that someone's intended action will be appropriate from a variety of viewpoints.

Kasperson *et al.* (1999) argue that the development of social trust is coextensive with the development of social capital. In their view, 'social capital comprises stocks of trust, norms of reciprocity and networks of civic engagement that make voluntary cooperation easier to attain. These stocks are "moral resources" that may be created and destroyed through "virtuous" or "vicious" circles' (1999: 30). They go on to argue that:

networks of civic engagement generate social capital by encouraging robust norms of reciprocity, reducing incentives to cheat, fostering communication (and thus reducing uncertainty about the trustworthiness of others) and building models of cooperation for use in the future.

Norms of reciprocity evolve because they lower transaction costs and cooperating individuals soon learn to trade off between long term altruism and short term self interest.

(Kasperson et al. 1999: 30–1)

Not surprisingly, social trust is presumably built slowly and increment-ally, it is probably never completely attained or attainable, it must be continually maintained and reinforced through networks of civic engage-ment and norms of reciprocity. In other words it is a two-way process, you cannot give it without its being received. For Kasperson *et al.* (1999: 37), social trust is multilayered:

[Trust] in the political system is onion like, with the deepest level, the core of the onion, being trust in the basic political community that includes the constitutional structure of politics and democratic institu-tions. Next is the layer of trust in the political regime, the norms and rules of the game that provide the context for democratic processes. Then comes trust in government and other political institutions. And finally there is the most superficial level of trust, that of particular representations of institutions.

Social trust is of two kinds: the pluralistic and the cosmopolitan (Earle and Cvetkovich, 1999). Pluralistic social trust is singular and rooted in the pasts of existing groups; because of this it is not useful in the management of complex social problems. Cosmopolitan social trust, on the other hand, is multiple, created in the emergence of new combinations of persons and groups. These new combinations are based on new sets of values that are constructed for the solution of specific problems (Earle and Cvetkovich 1999: 21). For current purposes, cosmopolitan social trust should stand at the core of an activist teacher professionalism. The solution to specific problems here will relate to aspects of practice and politics, which, at the macro and the micro levels, might impinge on practice.

Active trust

Active trust is not unconditional. It is not blind faith in other people but is a contingent and negotiated feature of professional or social engagement with others. As Giddens (1994) notes, active trust demands increased vis-ibility of social relations and also acts to increase such visibility. Recasting teacher professionalism in a more activist form calls for new kinds of social and professional relationships where different parts of the broader educa-tional enterprise work together in strategic ways. Rather than sectional interests working independently and sometimes in opposition, active trust requires that a shared set of values, principles and strategies is debated and negotiated. While on occasion it might be more strategic and in the interests of various sectional groups to act independently and autonomously, the larger political enterprise of defining notions of teacher professionalism and reclaiming moral and intellectual leadership over educational debates is the chief priority. David Hargreaves (1994: 424) claims that 'teachers are not merely working more co-operatively; they feel a stronger obligation towards and responsibility for their colleagues'. This sentiment is central for the generation and sustaining of active trust.

In activist professionalism, trust, obligation and solidarity work together in complementary ways. They are the cornerstones of engagement among the various interest groups. For Giddens (1994: 127):

> trust in personal relations depends on an assumption of the integrity of the other. It is based on a 'positive spiral' of difference. Getting to know the other, coming to rely on the other presumes pursuing difference as a means of developing positive emotional communication . . . Trust in others generates solidarity across time as well as space: the other is someone on whom one can rely, that reliance becoming a mutual obligation . . . When founded on active trust, obligation implies reciprocity. Obligations are binding because they are mutual, and this is what gives them their authority.

Active trust, respect and reciprocity stand at the core of an activist teacher professionalism. The challenge in becoming an activist professional is that it requires strong commitment of time, energy and intellectual resources to agree on what is at the core of the activism. Although it demands that each party should not inhabit the others' castles, as Somekh (1994) suggests, it does demand that each party at least looks inside the others' castles.

A further dimension of active trust is, as Fullan and Hargreaves (1992: 98) remind us, trust in processes. They argue that:

> Trust in expertise and processes helps organizations develop and solve problems on a continuing basis in an environment where problems and challenges are continuous and changing. Processes to be trusted here are ones that maximize the organization's collective expertise and improve its problem-solving capacities.

Central to the idea and the work of active trust is collaboration among various groups. Collaboration requires joint decision-making and new ways of working together. The Western Melbourne Roundtable is a group of five schools associated with the Innovative Links project in Melbourne, Victoria, that exemplifies this idea. The work of this team can be summarized as involving the processes of facilitation, collaboration and reflection. Team members act as facilitators in conducting workshops, organizing meetings and maintaining links with the Western Melbourne Roundtable. The school coordinator has a key role in organizing team meetings and communicating with school, university and teachers' union colleagues and collaborates with a university colleague sharing the tasks of facilitating case-writing workshops. Collaboration involves all team members in writing the cases, resolving questions about the style of case-writing and establishing relationships between colleagues from the schools, the university and the teachers' union. Talking about issues is an integral process as individuals are able to express their anxiety about how to go about case-writing, identify any difficulty in choosing a topic, and discuss ethical issues regarding recording personal information about children and experiences from the classroom. Finally, reflection on practice takes place informally through group discussion and individually through writing (Western Melbourne Roundtable 1996). Through its structures and processes this project typifies how decision-making is less hierarchical and requires different professional and personal relationships among various interest groups such as schools, universities, school systems, bureaucracies, unions and community groups. Nevertheless, this type of trust is risky and open-ended, but it is also essential to learning and improvement (Fullan and Hargreaves 1992).

As seen from the Western Melbourne Roundtable, collaborative partnerships involve a reciprocity that is in essence experimental. They assume that each party has something significant to contribute to the professional learning and political strategy of the other. They do, however, entail some risk, since they embody new relationships among the various parties and a different mode of operating within and outside traditional comfort zones. They also demonstrate that this kind of work is not apolitical and that it should be entered into with an understanding of the potential risks and controversies. Anderson and Herr (1999: 17) comment on the reciprocity and the implications of its practice, stating that:

> Academics who form alliances with practitioners or who send practitioners out into their schools to generate knowledge about practice should be equally willing to submit their own institutions and practices to the same level of investigative scrutiny.

Reciprocal forms of association have three purposes. First, all parties work towards building joint endeavours that are themselves concerned with promoting further collaborative development. In practice this could be the presentation of a joint paper at a conference, joint writing for publication or the development of collaborative research projects. Through such joint endeavours, all parties begin to understand and extend how each of them works in their various contexts, and they experience opportunities to exchange expertise. Second, by promoting collaborative development, school-based practitioners, academics, bureaucrats and union officials are all given the opportunity to elaborate practical theories. This enables and encourages them to examine the relationship between their espoused theories and their theories-in-use as they define and direct their separate and shared improvement efforts. In so doing, teachers and academics generate and sustain the energy for change within their evolving relationship. Finally, such practices enhance professional dialogue, generating analytical insights into and improvements of classroom practices in a variety of settings (Yeatman and Sachs 1995).

The project at Braidwood Central School, a K-10 school in rural New South Wales associated with the Innovative Links project, is illustrative of the importance of dialogue between teachers. The project at this school focused on developing a school culture that supported the establishment of a middle school department. Being part of the project enabled Braidwood Central School to develop links with other schools. It facilitated the development of a greater degree of colleagiality among staff and gave staff within the school opportunities to talk through issues with teachers from other schools associated with the project. In the words of one school staff member, 'Getting to talk to other people makes you have a good hard look at what you're doing'.

These new kinds of affiliation and collaboration move all parties beyond traditional technical notions of professional development and create spaces for new kinds of conversations to emerge. They provide opportunities for all groups to be engaged in public critical dialogues and debates about the nature of practice, how it can be communicated to others and how it can be continually improved. All parties move from peripheral involvement in the individual and collective projects to full participation. Dialogue is initiated about education in all of its contexts and dimensions, and about how people can learn from the experiences and collective wisdom of each other. At Braidwood the project provided staff with the confidence to implement change, and an opportunity to recognize the expertise that exists within the school (Southern Cross Roundtable Portrayal Evaluation Team 1996).

As projects like this develop, this dialogue becomes an integral part of the strategy for activating a community of activist professionals. It is ongoing, and while there are interruptions when the exigencies and pressures of life and work get in the way, the learning emerging from the dialogue can be returned to, reflected upon and provide the basis for new dialogues, positions and strategies. In the case of Braidwood, teachers spoke about how the project, in providing opportunities for release time and a collaborative relationship with university academics, gave them a sense of being valued and professional. For one member of staff this was the first time in a teaching career spanning 22 years that this sense of worth had been experienced. In another school the project opened up communication channels between teachers. Staff reported that the project had led to an enhancement of professional conversations between and among teaching staff:

> Prior to this we were faculty based but now a number of us work across faculties breaking down the boundaries ... we have spent a lot of time discussing educational issues rather than normal school time talk.
>
> (Currie *et al.* 1996: 40)

Under the conditions described here, expertise is interrogated and made mutually visible. As Giddens (1994: 129) notes: 'in a more reflexive social order, (existing) assumptions come under strain and start to break down'. Furthermore, as Giddens (1994: 129) suggests:

> as opposed to 'acceptance of', or 'reliance on', expert authority, active trust presumes visibility and responsibility on both sides. Reflexive engagements with abstract systems may be puzzling and disturbing for lay individuals and resented by professionals. Yet they force both to confront issues of responsibility that otherwise remain latent.

These are important aspects of active trust: it must be public and transparent, and it must be exercised collectively rather than individually. Sustaining active trust is time-consuming and demanding, but as the projects associated with the Innovative Links project demonstrate, the development of a collective strategy for improvement and learning is certainly worth this investment.

Generative politics

Generative politics complements and operationalizes a politics of transformation (see below). A fundamental feature of generative politics is that it allows and encourages individuals and groups to make things happen rather than to let things happen to them in the context of overall social concerns and goals. Generative politics exists in the space that links the state to reflexive mobilization in the society at large (Giddens 1994: 15). Furthermore, while generative politics is a defence of the politics of the public domain, it does not situate itself in the old opposition between state and market. Generative politics works through providing material conditions and organizational frameworks that enable people to take collective charge of their own destiny and life–political decisions in the wider social order (Giddens 1994). The interests of most importance are the most directly related to immediate and long-term issues which drive its goals and agendas. An agenda for a generative politics of teacher professionalism involves looking behind taken-for-granted assumptions about teacher professionalism and involves asking such questions as:

- Whose issues get put on the agenda and how do these issues become public?

- Who provides the initial moral and intellectual leadership in such an endeavour?
- How is inclusiveness promoted such that a broad range of educational interests is represented and heard?
- How can trust and understanding be established to overcome traditional suspicions and reservations?
- How can alternative forms of association at the local, national and global levels be established?
- How do we find new ways of engaging in action with an ever expanding group of interested parties, while remaining connected to our own place, time and interests?

Generative politics implies a number of conditions. First, it requires fostering the conditions under which desired outcomes can be achieved without determining those desires or bringing about those outcomes 'from the top'. In this respect, it is organic, since it develops spatially and temporally in response to local and global issues and the needs of those who are most directly involved and implicated. Second, generative politics involves creating situations in which *active trust* can be built and sustained, whether in schools, universities, bureaucracies or related agencies. Third, it demands according autonomy to those most affected by specific programmes or policies. In practice, this means that for generative politics to have the desired political outcomes it must emerge in response to real needs as they develop at the grassroots level. They cannot be imposed from outside by people who have little interest in the outcomes. Finally, decentralization of political power is crucial. According to Giddens (1994: 93): 'decentralisation is the condition of political effectiveness because of the requirement for bottom-up information flow as well as the recognition of autonomy'.

Social justice concerns are crucial for successful generative politics. They lead to a widened scope and increased levels of dialogue among various interested parties and through reflexivity and mutuality; they stimulate the production and dissemination of new knowledge and create opportunities for productive debate and engagement.

Generative politics provides an antidote to the fundamentalist and essentialist assumptions about social relations and organizations that inform managerialist notions of professionalism. Fundamentalist managerialist discourses of professionalism promote traditions and practices that have been appropriated from private sector management. The point about traditions, as Giddens (1994: 6) observes, is that 'you don't really have to justify them; they contain their own truth, a ritual truth, asserted as correct by the believer'. In a globally cosmopolitan order, such a stance becomes dangerous because it is a refusal of dialogue. The managerialist form of professionalism acts against generative politics and active trust. It segments and divides education interest groups and hinders rather than facilitates dialogue among them. It does not allow the development and facilitation of networks.

How, then, do we recognize an activist teacher professionalism that uses strategies to mobilize various constituencies derived from transformative and generative politics and which at the same time has a strong foundation in active trust? Drawing on my own and others' experiences of working in collegial and strategic ways with teachers, unions and systems to improve school-based practice, I now present a protocol for the aspiring activist teacher professional.

Politics of transformation

Activist teacher professionalism is in essence about a politics of transformation. Its spheres of interest are concerned with changing people's beliefs, perspectives and options regarding the importance of teaching, the social location of teachers and the role of competency and intelligent teachers in various education institutions. A politics of transformation is not self-interested; its concern is with wider issues of equity and social justice. Its focus is on the long rather than the short term, even though short-term gains are important in sustaining the energy and interest of participants. The politics of transformation is rooted in everyday life, and this is its strength. Cunningham *et al.* (1988) suggest that a politics of transformation challenges not only dominant interests but also the beliefs and practices that sustain power in everyday life: a politics that could thereby 'reflect and validate our role as agents of change rather than as simple victims in making the history' (cited in Carroll 1997: 7).

A politics of transformation requires various strategies to engage with and to change taken-for-granted assumptions about the role of education in society and the place of teachers within current and future education policy and practices. It requires new forms of collective identity, which not only transform people's self understandings but create cultural codes that contest the legitimacy of received points of view (Cohen 1985, cited in Carroll 1997). Individual and collective participation in a politics of transformation is concerned with engaging with the discursive practices that construct new political subjects and create new political spaces in which to act. This may ultimately lead people to rethink what they mean by community or power, or reason or democracy (Magnusson and Walker 1988). Furthermore, as Melucci (1988) claims, individuals and groups mount a symbolic challenge to the dominant codes, norms, identities and other sets of signs that regulate social life. As Masson (1997: 60) notes: 'this emphasises two main aspects. The first is the production of alternative frameworks of knowledge and meaning in the process of collective action. The second is the experimentation of new ways of living and new forms of relationships in the daily practice of movements' submerged networks'. The emphasis here is on the capacity of a new form of teacher professionalism to engage with and consequently reshape the discursive terrain of politics in distinctive and different ways. This can be achieved through personal and cultural transformations that run counter to existing orthodoxies or institutional formations. For teachers and people in the broader society it means rethinking the form, content and assumptions underpinning teacher professionalism and professional identity.

What, then, are the desired outcomes for a politics of transformation? First and foremost it means that there is a change of structures and processes around which debates about teacher professionalism take place. It means that oversight of structures that are currently in place to curtail teacher professional autonomy, such as standards boards and accreditation instrumentalities, are taken away from governments and given to teacher professional associations. Secondly, it requires that resources are made available so that this change may be achieved. Thirdly, it requires high levels of risk and trust on the part of all people associated with the endeavour. Finally, it requires the establishment of what might be called mobilizing structures such as networks to sustain the commitment and energy of members because it is the shared interests of members that underlie the process of mobilization as well as its sustainment.

A protocol for activist teacher professionalism

For my purposes here, a protocol refers to the way things are done and to the rituals and regulations that enable them to be done. The protocol has two dimensions: principles and practice. Given that activist teacher professionalism has roots in transformative and generative politics, developing a protocol for it requires new ways for teachers to work inside and outside of schools. It requires new kinds of affiliation and collaboration with various educational interest groups. A number of principles provide the foundation upon which any activist project needs to be grounded. These principles provide the strategic and conceptual scaffolding through which an activist teacher professionalism can be created and sustained. They include:

1 *Inclusiveness rather than exclusiveness.* This is crucial for the broad project of revitalizing teacher professionalism. Networks and partnerships are the mechanisms by which inclusiveness can be achieved and they should include teachers, academics, union officials, systems people, and employers as well as parents and other community groups. The broader the constituency and range of interests and expertise the greater the chance there is of mobilizing the interests of broad sectors of society.

2 *Collective and collaborative action.* People working individually can only do so much. Collective and collaborative action draws together a range of intellectual, social, cultural and other resources. Importantly, collaborative and collective action also helps to maintain energy levels and commitment. Interactions, sharing ideas and debating issues helps to sustain interest and works against disillusionment. It also helps to develop a more diverse range of strategies or conventions for collective action which individuals can draw upon at various times.

3 *Effective communication of aims and expectations.* The clear articulation of the aims and purposes of any political or group action is paramount. People need to know what is expected of them, what the risks and personal costs might be. While it is not possible to develop a definitive list of these, it is important to acknowledge that any form of collective action or transformative politics has attendant risks and costs.

4 *Recognition of the expertise of all parties involved.* Given the wide constituency of people interested in improving teaching, the work of teachers and the learning of students, there are likely to be participants with broad-ranging interests and expertise. The diversity of people's expertise is a resource to be taken advantage of and fostered. As the groups interested in an activist teacher or educational agenda will be drawn from a wide range of professions there will be opportunities for people to learn from each other and to develop their own skills as well as acquire new ones.

5 *Creating an environment of trust and mutual respect.* Activism requires trust in people and processes. Trust in times of passion and concerted collective efforts galvanize people. When trust erodes so too do the goodwill and energy that sustain any organization. It is important that there is the development of strategies and processes to support and reaffirm trust in the organization and trust in the strategies that are used to focus and mobilize action.

6 *Ethical practice.* This, in combination with acting ethically at all times, is fundamental to an activist teacher professional. Ethical practice relates to how people interact, how they communicate information and how they use information. It recognizes the needs, interests and sensitivities of various parties. In particular is the practice of cultural sensitivity and the acknowledgement that no researcher or activist is culturally neutral. At the core of ethical practice is the axiom of no harm to any party. Ethical practice is also mindful that relationships provide the glue for any form of transformative politics and that these must be nurtured and worked on, not taken for granted.

7 *Being responsive and responsible.* Timing in any form of collective action is important. Being mindful of strategy in the timing of meetings, the making of public statements and in utilizing the media is crucial. The

ability to read the strategic possibility of various situations is also important in order to take advantage of opportunities as they arise. Being responsible goes hand in hand with being responsive. Expedience or opportunism for self-promotion is best avoided. The best interests of the group should be at the forefront.

8 *Acting with passion.* Activism is not for the faint-hearted; it requires commitment, courage and determination. This kind of work involves high levels of emotional energy, it demands that participants believe strongly in their convictions and have the best interests of the group clearly in mind.

9 *Experiencing pleasure and having fun.* Last but not least, any form of activism must be pleasurable and there needs to be an element of fun in the activities, whether this is planning strategies for action, developing materials, or convincing others of the seriousness of the project. Indeed, while the intensity of the debate and the importance of the issues are to be taken seriously, the comradeship of fellow activists and the stories that develop about successes and failures all contribute to a broad sense of enjoyment in the endeavour. It is these stories and narratives that engender the sense of camaraderie of the group.

These principles are meant to be broad and flexible enough to sustain the momentum of what, at times, will be difficult political and professional work. They open up opportunities for renewing notions of teacher professionalism. They move beyond self-interested conceptions of professionalism which defend threatened interests, deny accusations of damning characteristics and claim only laudable characteristics (Freidson 1994: 171). Principles and practices of activist professionals, however, provide systematic ways of thinking and acting in the best of interests of *all* those involved in education. At the heart of these principles and practices are partnerships and practitioner research, or what I refer to as systematic enquiry, which in turn involves various processes of advocacy, network facilitation and mobilization. Networks and partnerships provide the structures for teacher activism to be supportive while systematic research provides a strategy and a process to achieve this.

Networks and partnerships

In any political endeavour involving different sectional or interest groups, reciprocity is crucial. Active listening and collective strategy is central to the successful implementation of any political activist project. Referring to school–university partnerships in particular, Yeatman (1996a) advocates a two-way partnership between teacher educators and practising teachers. She poses the question 'what can each of these partners offer to the other?'

This assumes a division of labour between the two partners where there is a difference through their respective roles and an articulation of this difference in the exchange of their respective skills and expertise (1996a: 24). According to Yeatman, such a partnership assumes that neither party can do its work adequately without the other's input. Accordingly, this exchange or partnership has to be integrated into the normal working arrangements of each partner's institution. Activist teacher professionalism across the whole profession (from primary schools to universities), requires that whole-school and individual capacities have to be incorporated into discussions with university teacher educators, union officials and systems and employing officials about strategy, processes and outcomes for improving teacher professionalism.

The political strategy of partnership work involves advocacy, network facilitation and mobilization. Partners who are activist professionals have, and are seen to have, intellectual and political resources and expertise that can be mobilized and harnessed whenever necessary. Significantly, it should also be recognized that, from time to time, each of the partners needs the autonomy and political space to act alone. On other occasions, though, as the need arises, partners will mobilize collectively and act in concert. At a time where 'teacher-bashing' is a national and international sport and when teacher shortages are imminent, it is crucial that stories of teacher and student success are written and circulated along with stories of local solidarity, trust and resistance. New alliances can be given voice and presence through the emergence of locally grounded social movements. Union participation in these can be developed. However, as Piven and Cloward (1979) concluded over twenty years ago, the success and failure of American social movements struggling for social change depended not on organizational prowess but on the ability to disrupt. Disruption and advocacy are complementary strategies. Advocacy is, in this respect, central to partnerships that embody and promote activist professionalism.

Networks are a second way for partners involved in education to direct the agenda of teacher professionalism. They derive great power and energy from offering members a voice in creating and sustaining a group in which their professional identity and interests are valued (Lieberman and Grolnick 1996). Networks of activist professionals sidestep the limitations of institutional roles, hierarchies and histories, and promote opportunities for diverse groups to work together. These networks can develop through already existing professional or industrial associations, or by coming together to review specific needs (being disestablished once their political project has been achieved), or by a slow and evolving process that requires continuing oversight and governance. The organization of the Innovative Links project through roundtables of five participating schools provided teachers with a range of opportunities to network with colleagues from other schools and to establish learning conversations. As the project became more established the learning conversations changed. As one teacher from Holy Eucharist Primary School in an outer suburb of Melbourne reflected:

> It was only when we started getting pieces of writing from the other schools that we started being able to have learning conversations. People were able to read about what was happening in the schools and ask questions about what was happening. We had an evening forum last year which started off with teachers talking about what schools had been doing. It changed from reporting to discussing what is happening and trying to work through substantial questions dealing with change.

When networks, coalitions and partnerships last long enough, they develop into ongoing learning communities, into deeply embedded cultures that are based on mutual knowledge, learning and collaboration. This replaces transmitting knowledge from one institution to another. When these cultures are focused on critical issues of school reform, they place educational practice at their centre, providing the kind of social and professional nourishment that leads many members to invest time, effort and commitment far beyond what they give to the usual professional development opportunities (Lieberman and Grolnick 1996: 41). Communities of critical friends develop during the course of the partnership work. In the case of the Innovative Links project, the role of the critical friend is often considered to be of greatest significance for teachers working with academic colleagues during the writing-up stage of action research projects. Currie *et al.* (1996: 11), in their evaluation of the second phase of the Innovative Links project, comment that:

> it is helpful (but not always comfortable) to have a critical friend who will challenge the assumptions on which the project is based, to clarify the language being used or to identify any contradictions in the proposed study . . . The process works most effectively where an atmosphere of trust develops between critical friends and members of the action research team.

Indeed the tension that sometimes emerges through the observations and interventions of a critical friend can be productive and lead to new insights and opportunities not previously apparent to other parties.

Systematic enquiry

Activist professionalism is founded not only on principles of mutual exchange, reciprocity and working together, but also on shared enquiry into patterns of practice. Such systematic enquiry is concerned with understanding and improving practice, and provides a way for teachers to come to know the epistemological bases of their practice. Following the work of Lawrence Stenhouse, it involves making teachers' work practices and learning public through systematic enquiry.

The experience of the National Schools Network (NSN) and Innovative Links project presented throughout this book has provided evidence for how systematic enquiry by teachers with support from university colleagues can enable them to ask critical questions about their practice and to undertake systematic means of enquiry in order to understand or improve their practice.

The professional and political project of systematic teacher enquiry and collaborative partnerships is to move professional and public discourses about schooling beyond traditional technical notions of professional development, such as in-service training, and create spaces for new kinds of conversations to emerge. They provide opportunities for academics and school-based colleagues to engage in public critical debates about the nature of practice, how it can be communicated with others and how it can be continually improved. These activities not only underpin an activist teacher professionalism but also help to embed it into the work of teachers and the expectations that the community has about what is means to be a professional.

Such activist teacher professionalism calls for more than just new kinds of teachers in new school cultures and structures. It also calls for new kinds of teacher educators, new cultures in schools of education, and altered university structures for academics. Changing the culture and structure of the schools may look like a difficult task, but it is not impossible (Soltis 1994: 255). The same can be said for teacher education. How this might be done was outlined in Chapter 4. An activist teacher professionalism will also require new forms of affiliation and association between systems and union officials, as well as opportunities for all parties to come together on 'neutral' ground that has not been tainted by previous experiences, prejudices and leftover ideological baggage.

For teachers, activist professionalism means reinventing their professional identity and how they define themselves as teachers within their own schools and the wider education community. It means that they rethink their social relationships and pedagogical practices within and outside of schools. This is no small task, as it means questioning and shedding previously cherished values and beliefs. Similarly for teacher educators, activist professionalism requires personal and professional changes. This reinventing is along the lines of what Liston and Zeichner (1991) describe as social reconstructionist teacher educators. According to them (1991: 188), social reconstructionist teacher educators should be:

- directly involved in a teacher education programme in some capacity;
- engaged in political work within colleges and universities;
- actively supportive of efforts within public [state] schools to create more democratic work and learning environments;
- engaged within professional associations and in relation to state education agencies;
- working for democratic changes aimed at achieving greater social justice in other societal and political arenas.

For union officials and people working in educational bureaucracies, activist professionalism demands that they develop new strategies for communicating with their constituencies. These strategies should be collegial, respectful and tactical. Finally, for parents and other community members, activism means that they feel confident to work with other groups such as teachers, teacher educators, unionists and bureaucrats in inclusive and reciprocal ways.

The future challenge then is to create the political and professional conditions where new cultures can emerge and be sustained in schools, education bureaucracies and faculties of education in which teacher research is rewarded and respected instead of being placed at the margins of university priorities. This type of work exemplifies the work of activist professionals working in situ.

Conclusion

Activist teacher professionalism anticipates that teachers and others who are interested in education will be able to defend and understand themselves better. As Bottery (1996) argues, this activist orientation comes from educators understanding not only their practice, but also themselves in relation to the society in which they live. Activist teacher professionalism is not for the faint-hearted. It requires risk-taking and working collectively and tactically with others. Like any form of action it demands conviction and strategy. However, the benefits outweigh the demands. The activist teacher professional creates new spaces for action and debate, and in so doing improves the learning opportunities for all of those who are recipients or providers of education.

The development of a transformative politics to facilitate an activist teacher professionalism requires both short-term and long-term goals and activities which in turn will promote immediate and future-oriented gains. Such strategies need to be developed by members of the group itself because they will have no currency among members if they are imposed from outside the group.

The experiences of teachers and others reported in this book demonstrate the power of grassroots and local school and profession-oriented strategies. For interest and passion to be sustained, the activist project must be local in its focus, but at the same time some implications regarding changing practice or educational innovation may have more widespread application.

There are many lessons to be learnt from the work of teachers currently working along activist lines. Unfortunately, their efforts, successes and the stories of their work are known only to a few. The future challenge will be to find various means to communicate to wider audiences of practitioners and non-practitioners alike, the outcomes of what is often challenging, difficult, but worthwhile work.

It is hoped that by telling stories of teachers' and students' achievements, other teachers will be inspired to extend their own work along activist lines. No one has said this will be easy, but who could resist the challenge to reinvigorate and make a difference to the teaching profession? The evidence of other social movements suggests that identifying achievable goals, communicating these to the membership, and utilizing strategic planning and thinking in order to achieve those goals, does pay off. In this case the stakes are high but the rewards are great. If we want to build a new form of teacher professionalism then we should take our inspiration from those many teachers who are making a difference to the lives of the children they teach.

I finish with a call to action. An activist teaching profession is an educated and politically astute one. The will to achieve this is lying dormant in many of us, and now is the time to work towards its development and realization in systematic and collective ways. Teachers in individual schools can work at the school level, regionally, or, as some of the examples presented here, at the national level, to achieve socially responsible goals. Teacher educators, bureaucrats, unionists and others interested in education also need to join together in order to make public and to celebrate the achievements of teachers. They also need strategies to inform those in positions of power and influence of the importance and necessity of a strong teaching profession. It is this kind of profession that can educate our children to be socially active and responsible citizens. There is no time to lose. We can frame the future agendas for schooling and education, we just need to harness the various intellectual, social and political resources available to us in order to achieve it.

References

ACIIC Roundtable, University of Sydney (1996) *Reflection in Action*, Report of the Evaluation of the Innovative Links Project. Perth: Murdoch University.

Altrichter, H. Posch, P. and Somekh, B. (1993) *Teachers Investigate their Work: An Introduction into Methods of Action Research*. London: Routledge.

Anderson, G. and Herr, K. (1999) The new paradigm war: is there room for rigorous practitioner knowledge in schools and universities?, *Education Researcher*, 28(2): 12–21.

Andrew, M. (1997) What matters most to teacher educators, *Journal of Teacher Education*, 48(3): 167–76.

Angus, M. (1996) Award restructuring in schools: educational idealism versus political pragmatism, in T. Seddon (ed.) *Pay, Professionalism and Politics: Reforming Teachers, Reforming Education*. Melbourne: Australian Council for Educational Research.

Apple, M. (1982) *Education and Power*. Boston: Routledge & Kegan Paul.

Apple, M. (1993) *Official Knowledge: Democratic Education in a Conservative Age*. New York: Teachers College Press.

Apple, M. (1996) *Cultural Politics and Education*. New York: Teachers College Press.

Apple, M. (2000) *Official Knowledge: Democratic Education in a Conservative Age*, 2nd edn. New York: Routledge.

Apple, M. (2001) *Educating the Right Way*. London: Routledge.

Apple, M. and Beane, J. (1999) *Democratic Schools: Lessons from the Chalkface*. Buckingham: Open University Press.

Atkinson, E. (2000) In defense of ideas, or what works is not enough, *British Journal of Sociology of Education*, 21(3): 318–30.

Atkinson, T. and Claxton, G. (eds) (1999) *The Intuitive Practitioner*. Buckingham: Open University Press.

Ball, S. (1994) *Educational Reform: A Critical Post-structural Approach*. Buckingham: Open University Press.

Ball, S. (1995) Intellectuals or technicians: the urgent role of theory in educational studies, *British Journal of Educational Studies*, 43(2): 255–71.

Beane, J. and Apple, M. (1995) The case for democratic schools, in M. Apple and J. Beane *Democratic Schools*. Victoria: ASCD.

Beattie, M. (1995) New prospects for teacher education: narrative ways of knowing teaching and teacher learning, *Education Research*, 37(1): 53–70.

Bernstein, B. (1996) *Pedagogy, Symbolic Control and Identity*. London: Taylor & Francis.

Bottery, M. (1996) The challenge to professionals from the new public management: implications for the teaching profession, *Oxford Review of Education*, 22(2): 179–97.

Bottery, M. and Wright, N. (2000) *Teachers and the State*. London: Routledge.

Bradbury, J., Branch, K. and Focht, W. (1999) Trust and public participation in risk policy issues, in G. Cvetkovich and R. Lofstedt (eds) *Social Trust and the Management of Risk*. London: Earthscan.

Brennan, M. (1996) *Multiple Professionalisms for Australian Teachers in an Information Age*. New York: American Education Research Association.

Brennan, M. and Sachs, J. (1998) *Integrated Curriculum: Classroom Materials for the Middle Years of Schooling*. Deakin West, ACT: ACSA/NSN.

Brint, S. (1994) *In an Age of Experts: The Changing Role of Professionals in Politics and Public Life*. Princeton, NJ: Princeton University Press.

Burrow, S. (1996) Award restructuring: the teaching profession, in T. Seddon (ed.) *Pay, Professionalism and Politics*. Melbourne: Australian Council for Educational Research.

Carroll, W. (1997) Social movements and counter hegemony: Canadian context and social theories, in W. Carroll (ed.) *Organizing Dissent: Contemporary Social Movements in Theory and Practice*. Toronto: Garamond Press.

Carter, K. and Halsall, R. (1998) Teacher research for school improvement, in R. Halsall (ed.) *Teacher Research and School Improvement: Opening the Doors from the Inside*. Buckingham: Open University Press.

Casey, C. (1995) *Work, Self and Society: After Industrialism*. London: Routledge.

Casey, K. (1993) *I Answer with My Life: Life Histories of Women Teachers Working for Social Change*. London: Routledge.

Castells, M. (1997) *The Power of Identity*. Oxford: Basil Blackwell.

Chadbourne, R. (1999) Australian views on the American National Board standards for early childhood teachers, *Unicorn*, 25(2): 37–59.

Clandinin, J. and Connelly, M. (1988) *Teachers as Curriculum Planners: Narratives of Experience*. New York: Teacher College Press.

Clandinin, J. and Connelly, M. (eds) (1995) *Teachers' Professional Knowledge Landscapes*. New York: Teacher College Press.

Clarke, J. (1995) Doing the right thing: managerialism and social welfare. Paper presented to the Social Policy Association, University of Nottingham, July.

Clarke, J. and Newman, J. (1997) *The Managerial State*. London: Sage.

Cochran-Smith, M. and Lytle, S. (1998) Teacher research: the question that persists, *International Journal of Leadership in Education*, 1(1): 19–36.

Cunningham, F., Findlay, S., Kadar, M., Lennon, A. and Silva, E. (eds) *1988 Social Movements/Social Change: The Politics and Practice of Organizing*. Toronto, ON: Between the Lines.

Currie, J. and Groundwater Smith, S. (1998) *Learning is When: Kids Help Teachers, Kids Help Kids, Teachers Help Kids, Kids Help Teachers.* Sydney: Australian Schools Network.

Currie, J., Davey, M., Grant, M. *et al.* (1996) *Innovating and Changing Together.* Sydney: Australian Schools Network.

Cvetkovich, G. and Lofstedt, R. (1999) *Social Trust and the Management of Risk.* London: Earthscan.

Czarniawska, B. (1997) *Narrating the Organization.* Chicago: University of Chicago Press.

Dadds, M. (1995) *Passionate Inquiry and School Development: A Story of Teacher Action.* London: Falmer Press.

Dadds, M. and Hart, S. (2001) *Doing Practitioner Research Differently.* London: Falmer/Routledge.

Dalin, P. (1996) Can schools learn? preparing for the 21st century, NASSP *Bulletin,* 80(576): 9–15.

Darling Hammond, L. (1998) Policy and change: getting beyond bureaucracy, in A. Hargreaves, A. Lieberman, M. Fullan and D. Hopkins (eds), *International Handbook of Educational Change.* Amsterdam: Kluwer.

Darling Hammond, L. (1999) *Reshaping Teaching Policy, Preparation and Practice: Influences on the National Board for Teaching Professional Standards.* Washington, DC: AACTE Publications.

Day, C. (1999) *Developing Teachers: The Challenges of Lifelong Learning.* London: Falmer Press.

Day, C., Fernandez, A., Hauge, T. and Moller, J. (eds) (2000) *The Life and Work of Teachers.* London: Falmer Press.

Delor, J. (1996) *Learning the Treasure that Lies Within.* Paris: UNESCO.

Dewey, J. (1916) *Democracy and Education.* New York: Macmillan.

DfEE (Department of Education and Employment) (1997) *Teaching: High Status, High Standards,* Circular 10/97. London: DfEE.

Drucker, P. (1994) The age of social transformation, *The Atlantic Monthly,* 274(5): 53–80.

du Gay, P. (1996) *Consumption and Identity at Work.* London: Sage.

Earle, T. and Cvetkovich, G. (1999) Social trust and culture in risk management, in G. Cvetkovich and R. Lofstedt (eds) *Social Trust and the Management of Risk.* London: Earthscan.

Elbaz, F. (1983) *Teacher Thinking: A Study of Practical Knowledge.* London: Croom Helm.

Elliott, J. (1991) *Action Research for Educational Change.* Buckingham: Open University Press.

Epstein, A. (1978) *Ethos and Identity.* London: Tavistock.

Etzioni, A. (1996) *The New Golden Rule: Community and Morality in a Democratic Society.* New York: Basic Books.

Ewing, R. and Smith, D. (1999) *Preparing Australia's Teachers for the 21st Century: The Master of Teaching Experience.* Montreal: AERA.

Exworthy, M. and Halford, S. (1999) *Professionalism and the New Managerialism in the Public Sector.* Buckingham: Open University Press.

Fergusson, R. (1994) Managerialism and education, in J. Clarke, A. Cochrane, E. Mclaughlin *et al.* (eds) *Managing Social Policy.* London: Sage.

Freidson, E. (1986) *Professional Powers: A Study of the Institutionalization of Formal Knowledge*. Chicago: University of Chicago Press.

Freidson, E. (1994) *Professionalism Reborn*. Chicago: University of Chicago Press.

Fukuyama, F. (1999) *The Great Disruption: Human Nature and the Reconstitution of Social Order*. New York: Touchstone Books.

Fullan, M. (1993) *Change Forces*. London: Falmer Press.

Fullan, M. and Hargreaves, A. (1992) *What's Worth Fighting for In Your School?* Buckingham: Open University Press.

Fullan, M., Galluzzo, G., Morris, M. and Watson, N. (1998) *The Rise and Stall of Teacher Education Reform*. Washington, DC: American Association of Colleges of Teacher Education.

Furlong, J., Barton, L., Miles, S. Whiting, C. and Whitty, G. (2000) *Teacher Education in Transition*. Buckingham: Open University Press.

Gee, J., Hull, G. and Lankshear, C. (1996) *The New Work Order: Behind the Language of New Capitalism*. Sydney: Allen & Unwin.

Gergen, K. and Gergen, M. (1988) Narrative and the self as relationship, in L. Berkowitz (ed.) *Advances in Experimental Social Psychology 21*. New York: Academic Press.

Gerstein, A. (1999) *Principles at Work: Measuring the Success of the Coalition of Essential Schools 1999–2000*, ERIC Document No. 439 511.

Giddens, A. (1994) *Beyond Left and Right: The Future of Radical Politics*. Oxford: Polity Press.

Goodlad, J. (1984) *A Place Called School*. New York: McGraw-Hill.

Goodson, I. (1999) The educational researcher as public intellectual, *British Education Research Journal*, 25(3): 277–98.

Goodson, I. and Hargreaves, A. (1996) *Teachers' Professional Lives*. London: Falmer Press.

Grace, G. (1987) Teachers and the state in Britain: a changing relationship, in M. Lawn and G. Grace (eds) *Teachers: The Culture and Politics of Work*. London: Falmer Press.

Greene, M. (1995) *Releasing the Imagination: Essays on Education, the Arts and Social Change*. San Franciso: Jossey-Bass.

Grenfell, M. and Clancy, J. (1998) *The Northern Link: Action Research in Top End Schools*. Darwin: Northern Territory University.

Grimmett, P. (1995) Reconceptualizing teacher education: preparing teachers for revitalized schools, in M. Wideen, and P. Grimmett (eds) *Changing Times in Teacher Education: Restructuring or Reconceptualization?* London: Falmer Press.

Groundwater Smith, S. (1996) Putting Teacher Professional Judgement to Work. Paper presented at the Practitioner Research and Academic Practices Conference, Fitzwilliam College, Cambridge.

Groundwater Smith, S. (2001) Supporting and Sustaining the Knowledge Building School. Paper presented to the European Educational Research Association Annual Conference, Lille, France, 5–8 September.

Gutmann, A. and Thompson, D. (1996) *Democracy and Disagreement*. Cambridge, MA: Belknap Press.

Halsall, R. (1998) *Teacher Research and School Improvement: Opening Doors from the Inside*. Buckingham: Open University Press.

Hanlon, C. (1998) Professionalism as enterprise: service class politics and the redefinition of professionalism, *Sociology*, 32(1): 43–63.

Hargreaves, A. (1992) The cultures of teaching, in A. Hargreaves and M. Fullan (eds) *Understanding Teacher Development*. New York: Teachers College Press.

Hargreaves, A. (1994) *Changing Teachers, Changing Time*. New York: Teachers College Press.

Hargreaves, A. (2000) Four ages of professionalism and professional learning, *Teachers and Teaching: Theory and Practice*, 6(2): 151–82.

Hargreaves, A. and Fullan, M. (1992) *Understanding Teacher Development*. New York: Teachers College Press.

Hargreaves, A. and Goodson, I. (1996) Teachers' professional lives: aspirations and actualities, in I. Goodson and A. Hargreaves (eds) *Teachers' Professional Lives*. London: Falmer Press.

Hargreaves, D. (1994) The new professionalism: the synthesis of professional and institutional development, *Teaching and Teacher Education*, 10(4): 423–38.

Hargreaves, D. (1999) The knowledge creating school, *British Journal of Education Studies*, 47: 122–44.

Helsby, G. (1999) *Changing Teachers' Work*. Buckingham: Open University Press.

Hollingsworth, S. and Sockett, H. (1994) Teacher research and educational reform, in H. Sockett and S. Hollingsworth (eds) *Teacher Research and Educational Reform*. Chicago: University of Chicago Press.

Hoyle, E. and John, P. (1995) *Professional Knowledge and Professional Practice*. New York: Cassell.

Huberman, M. (1996) Focus on research moving mainstream: taking a closer look at teacher research, *Language Arts*, 73: 124–40.

Ingvarson, L. (1998a) *A Professional Development System Fit for a Profession*, IARVT Seminar Series, No. 72, Victoria.

Ingvarson, L. (1998b) Professional standards: a challenge for AATE, *English in Australia*, 122: 31–44.

Ingvarson, L. (1998c) Teaching standards: foundations for professional development reform, in A. Hargreaves, A. Lieberman, M. Fullan, and D. Hopkins (eds) *International Handbook of Educational Change*. Amsterdam: Kluwer.

Ingvarson, L. (1999) The power of professional recognition, *Unicorn*, 25(2): 60–71.

Jackson, P. (1968) *Life in Classrooms*. New York: Holt, Rinehart & Winston.

Johnson, S. Moore (2000) Can professional certification for teachers reshape teaching as a career? Implementing change in the US, *Unicorn*, 26(1): 21–32.

Kasperson, R., Golding, D. and Kasperson, J. (1999) Risk, trust and democratic theory, in G. Cvetkovich and R. Lofstedt (eds) *Social Trust and the Management of Risk*. London: Earthscan.

Kenway, J., Bigum, C., Fitzclarence, L. and Collier, J. (1993) Marketing education in the 1990s: an introductory essay, *Australian Universities Review*, 36(2): 2–6.

Kondo, D. (1990) *Crafting Selves*. Chicago: University of Chicago Press.

Ladwig, J. and White, V. (1996) Integrating research and development in the National Schools Network, *Australian Journal of Education*, 40(3): 302–10.

Ladwig, J., Currie, J. and Chadbourne, R. (1995) *Towards Rethinking Australian Schools*. Sydney: National Schools Network.

Larson, M. (1977) *The Rise of Professionalism: A Sociological Analysis.* Berkeley: University of California Press.

Larson, M. (1993) *Behind the Postmodern Façade.* Berkeley: University of California Press.

Lave, J. and Wenger, E. (1991) *Situated Learning: Legitimate Peripheral Participation.* Cambridge: Cambridge University Press.

Lieberman, A. and Grolnick, M. (1996) Networks and reform in American education, *Teachers College Record*, 98(1): 7–45.

Lipset, S.M. and Schneider, W. (1987) *The Confidence Gap: Business, Labour and Government in the Public Mind.* New York: Macmillan.

Liston, D. and Zeichner, K. (1991) *Teacher Education and the Social Conditions of Schooling.* New York: Routledge.

Lockwood, A. (1998) *Comprehensive Reform: A Guide for School Leaders.* www.ncrel.org/cscd/pubs/lead52/52qlltxt.htm (accessed Oct. 2001)

Lortie, D. (1975) *Schoolteacher: A Sociological Study.* Chicago: University of Chicago Press.

Louden, W. (1999) Standards for standards: an Australian perspective on the development and assessment of professional standards. Paper presented to the New Professionalism in Teaching, Teacher Education and Teacher Development in A Changing World Conference, Hong Kong, 13–16 January.

Lytle, S. and Cochran-Smith, M. (1994) Inquiry, Knowledge and Practice, in S. Hollingsworth and H. Sockett (eds) *Teacher Research and Educational Reform*, Ninety-third Yearbook of the National Society for the Study of Education. Chicago: University of Chicago Press.

Macdonald, K. (1995) *The Sociology of the Professions.* Thousand Oaks, CA: Sage.

Magnusson, W. and Walker, R. (1988) Decentering the state: political theory and Canadian political economy, *Studies in Political Economy*, 26: 37–71.

Mahony, P. and Hextall, I. (2000) *Reconstructing Teaching: Standards, Performance and Accountability.* London: Routledge/Falmer.

Marginson, S. (1997) *Markets in Education.* Sydney: Allen & Unwin.

Masson, D. (1997) Language, power and politics: revisiting the symbolic challenge of movements, in W. Carroll (ed.) *Organizing Dissent: Contemporary Social Movements in Theory and Practice.* Toronto: Garamond Press.

McCulloch, G., Helsby, G. and Knight, P. (2000) *The Politics of Professionalism.* London: Continuum.

McLaughlin, M. (1997) Rebuilding teacher professionalism in the United States, in A. Hargreaves and R. Evans (eds) *Beyond Educational Reform.* Buckingham: Open University Press.

Melucci, A. (1988) Social movements and the democratization of social life, in J. Keane (ed.) *Civil Society and the State.* London: Verso.

Melucci, A. (1996) *The Playing Self: Persons and Meaning in the Planetary Society.* Cambridge: Cambridge University Press.

Menter, I., Muschamp, Y., Nicolls, P., Ozga, J. and Pollard, A. (1997) *Work and Identity in the Primary School.* Buckingham: Open University Press.

Millett, A. (1997) Letter to *Providers*, 26 June.

Misztal, B. (1996) *Trust in Modern Societies: The Search for the Basis of Social Order.* Cambridge: Polity Press.

Nee, E.J. (1999) Systematic risk-taking. Paper presented to the Teach to Reach Conference, Teachers' Network, Singapore, 26–30 April.

Nias, J., Southworth, G. and Yeomans, R. (1989) *Staff Relations in the Primary School*. London: Cassell.

Noffke, S. (1997) Professional, personal and political aspects of action research, *Review of Research in Education*, 23. Washington, DC: AERA.

OECD (1995) *Governance in Transition: Public Management Reform in OECD Countries*. Paris: OECD.

Ozga, J. and Lawn, M. (1981) *Teachers, Professionalism and Class: A Study of Organized Teachers*. Lewes: Falmer Press.

Piven, F. and Cloward, R. (1979) *Poor People's Movements: Why They Succeed, How They Fail*. New York: Vintage.

Pollitt, C. (1990) *Managerialism and the Public Services: The Anglo-American Experience*. Oxford: Basil Blackwell.

Power, M. (1997) *The Audit Society: Rituals of Verification*. Oxford: Oxford University Press.

Preston, B. (1996) Award restructuring: a catalyst in the evolution of teacher professionalism, in T. Seddon (ed.) *Pay, Professionalism and Politics*. Melbourne: Australian Council for Educational Research.

Putnam, R. and Borko, H. (1997) Teacher learning: implications of new views of cognition, in B. Biddle, T. Good and I. Goodson (eds) *International Handbook of Teachers and Teaching*. Dordrecht: Kluwer.

Rees, S. (1995) The fraud and the fiction, in S. Rees, and G. Rodley (eds) *The Human Costs of Managerialism*. Sydney: Pluto Press.

Reid, A., McCallum, F. and Dobbins, R. (1998) Teachers as political actors, *Asia Pacific Journal of Teacher Education*, 26(3): 247–59.

Sachs, J. (1997) Reinventing teacher professionalism, *Journal of Education for Teaching*, 23(3): 253–75.

Sachs, J. (1999) Using teacher research as a basis for professional renewal, *Journal of Inservice Education*, 25(1): 39–53.

Sachs, J. (2000) The activist professional, *Journal of Educational Change*, 1(1): 77–95.

Sachs, J. and Logan, L. (1997) Musings on the future of primary schooling, in L. Logan and J. Sachs (eds) *Meeting the Challenges of Primary Schooling*. London: Routledge.

Schratz, M. and Walker, R. (1995) *Research as Social Change: New Opportunities for Qualitative Research*. London: Routledge.

Seddon, T. (1996) *Pay, Professionalism and Politics: Reforming Teachers, Reforming Education*. Melbourne: Australian Council for Educational Research.

Senate Employment, Education and Training Reference Committee (1998) *A Class Act – Inquiry into the status of the Teaching Profession*. Canberra: Australian Government Publishing Service.

Sergiovani, T. (1998) Markets and community strategies for change: what works best for deep changes in schools, in A. Hargreaves, A. Lieberman, M. Fullan and D. Hopkins (eds) *International Handbook for Educational Change*. Amsterdam: Kluwer.

Shulman, L. (1986) Those who understand: knowledge growth in teaching, *Educational Researcher*, 15(2): 4–14.

Simon, K. and Gerstein, A. (n.d.) The Coalition of Essential Schools: a principle based approach to school reform. www.essentialschools.org/aboutus/phil/chapter/ceschapter.html (accessed Oct. 2001)

Sinclair, A. (1995) Leadership in administration: rediscovering a lost discourse, in P. Weller and G. Davis (eds) *New Ideas, Better Government*. St Leonards, NSW: Allen & Unwin.

Smith, R. (2000) The future of teacher education: principles and prospects, *Asia Pacific Journal of Teacher Education*, 28(1): 7–28.

Smith, R. and Weaver, C. (1998) The end of teacher education: strong signal and weak directions. *Change: Transformations in Education*, 1(1): 32–47.

Smyth, J., Dow, A., Hattam, R., Reid, A. and Schacklock, G. (2000) *Teachers' Work in a Globalizing Economy*. London: Falmer Press.

Soltis, J. (1994) The new teacher, in H. Sockett and S. Hollingsworth (eds) *Teacher Research and Educational Reform*. Chicago: University of Chicago Press.

Somekh, B. (1994) Inhabiting each other's castles: towards knowledge and mutual growth though collaboration, *Education Action Research*, 2(3): 357–80.

Southern Cross Roundtable Portrayal Evaluation Team (1996) *Partners in Research: Teachers and Teacher Educators Learning Together*. Perth: Murdoch University.

Suan, W.L. (1999) Problem-solving: the holistic approach. Paper presented to the Teach to Reach Conference, Teachers' Network, Singapore, 26–30 April.

Sykes, G. (1990) Fostering teacher professionalism in schools, in R. Elmore (ed.) *Restructuring Schools: The Next Generation of Educational Reform*. San Francisco: Jossey-Bass.

Tarrow, S. (1996) *Power in Movement: Social Movements, Collective Action and Politics*. Cambridge: Cambridge University Press.

Taylor, S., Rizvi, F., Lingard, B. and Henry, M. (1997) *Educational Policy and the Politics of Change*. New York: Routledge.

Tedesco, J. (1996). The role of teachers, *Educational Innovation*, 88 (September): 1.

Thiessen, D. (1992) Classroom based teacher development, in A. Hargreaves and M. Fullan (eds) *Understanding Teacher Development*. New York: Teachers College Press.

Thuraisingam, P. (1999) The interpretive role of the history teacher in a knowledge-based economy. Paper presented to the Humanities Conference: The Humanities Teacher in a Knowledge-based Economy, Conference sponsored by the Teachers' Network, Singapore, 2–6 March.

Tom, A. (1997) *Redesigning Teacher Education*. Albany: State University of New York Press.

Troman, G. (1996) The rise of the new professionals? The restructuring of primary teachers' work and professionalism, *British Journal of Sociology of Education*, 17(4): 473–97.

TTA (Teacher Training Agency) (1998) *Initial Teacher Training: Performance Profiles*. London: TTA.

Wenger, E. (1998) *Communities of Practice: Learning, Meaning and Identity*. Cambridge: Cambridge University Press.

Western Melbourne Roundtable (1996) *Teachers Write: A Handbook for Teachers Writing about Changing Classrooms for a Changing World*. Sydney: National Schools Network.

Whitty, G. (2000) Teacher professionalism in new times, *Journal of Inservice Education*, 26(2): 281–96.
Whitty, G., Power, S. and Halpin, D. (1998) *Devolution and Choice in Education*. Buckingham: Open University Press.
Yeatman, A. (1996a) Building effective school–university partnerships, *Forum of Education*, 51(2): 21–32.
Yeatman, A. (1996b) Managing the politics of uncertainty. Paper presented to the Reform Agendas Conference, Making Education Work, University of Sydney.
Yeatman, A. and Sachs, J. (1995) *Making the Links: A Formative Evaluation of the First Year of the Innovative Links between Universities and Schools for Teacher Professional Development*. Perth: Murdoch University.

Index

Page numbers in *italic* refer to main discussion, *n* indicates a note.

TEACHER LEARNING FOR EDUCATIONAL CHANGE
A SYSTEMS THINKING APPROACH

Garry F. Hoban

Hoban pays careful attention to the dynamic interplay between personal, social and contextual conditions for learning in his Professional Learning System by valuing extended time frames and learning communities in his quest for real teacher change. But beyond his theory, persuasive arguments and compelling examples is the learning through reflection that he embodies himself in this book. A wonderful read.

J. John Loughran, Faculty of Education,
Monash University, Australia

How many teachers (including academics) understand the dynamic relationship between learning and teaching? In this highly readable account of teacher learning for educational change, Hoban provides both the theory and the detailed examples for a rich and engaging new perspective on teachers' professional learning. This is essential reading for all who would improve their own teaching or provide meaningful support and leadership for such teachers.

Tom Russell, Professor of Education,
Queen's University, Canada

This book presents a new mindset for teacher learning and educational change. When viewed from a conventional mechanistic paradigm, educational change is a linear step-by-step process that is supported by a simplistic approach to teacher learning. Although this approach often produces disappointing results, rarely is an alternative one proposed. What is new in this book is that educational change and teacher learning are viewed from a paradigm based on complexity theory, assuming that change is a nonlinear process that needs to be supported by a framework for long-term teacher learning. The central question of this book, therefore, is 'What conditions will help to establish a framework for long-term teacher learning to support educational change?' To address this question, a systems thinking approach is used to draw together ideas from existing learning perspectives into a new theoretical framework called a Professional Learning System. This framework is not a formula, but a new mindset to help us understand the nonlinear dynamics of educational change and teacher learning.

Contents

208pp   0 335 20953 X (Paperback)   0 335 20954 8 (Hardback)

Whitty, G. (2000) Teacher professionalism in new times, *Journal of Inservice Education*, 26(2): 281–96.

Whitty, G., Power, S. and Halpin, D. (1998) *Devolution and Choice in Education*. Buckingham: Open University Press.

Yeatman, A. (1996a) Building effective school–university partnerships, *Forum of Education*, 51(2): 21–32.

Yeatman, A. (1996b) Managing the politics of uncertainty. Paper presented to the Reform Agendas Conference, Making Education Work, University of Sydney.

Yeatman, A. and Sachs, J. (1995) *Making the Links: A Formative Evaluation of the First Year of the Innovative Links between Universities and Schools for Teacher Professional Development*. Perth: Murdoch University.

Index

Page numbers in *italic* refer to main discussion, *n* indicates a note.